HENRI NOUWEN

MODERN SPIRITUAL MASTERS
Robert Ellsberg, Series Editor

This series introduces the writing and vision of some of the great spiritual masters of the twentieth century. Along with selections from their writings, each volume includes a comprehensive introduction, presenting the author's life and writings in context, and drawing attention to points of special relevance to contemporary spirituality.

Some of these authors found a wide audience in their lifetimes. In other cases recognition has come long after their deaths. Some are rooted in long-established traditions of spirituality. Others charted new, untested paths. In each case, however, the authors in this series have engaged in a spiritual journey shaped by the influences and concerns of our age. Such concerns include the challenges of modern science, religious pluralism, secularism, and the quest for social justice.

At the dawn of a new millennium this series commends these modern spiritual masters, along with the saints and witnesses of previous centuries, as guides and companions to a new generation of seekers.

Already published:
Dietrich Bonhoeffer (edited by Robert Coles)
Simone Weil (edited by Eric O. Springsted)

Forthcoming volumes include:
Pierre Teilhard de Chardin
Karl Rahner
Oscar Romero
John Main
Flannery O'Connor
Brother Roger of Taizé

MODERN SPIRITUAL MASTERS SERIES

HENRI NOUWEN

*Writings Selected
with an Introduction by*

ROBERT A. JONAS

ORBIS BOOKS

Maryknoll, New York 10545

Library of Congress Cataloging-in-Publication Data
Nouwen, Henri J. M.
    [Selections. 1998]
    Henri Nouwen : writings / selected with an introduction by Robert A. Jonas.
        p. cm. – (Modern spiritual masters series)
    ISBN 1-57075-197-8 (pbk.)
    1. Christian life – Catholic authors.   I. Jonas, Robert A.
II. Title.   III. Series.
BX2350.2.N67 1998
248.4'82 – dc21   98-38591

Contents

Acknowledgments

What an exciting opportunity and privilege it has been to write about my friend and mentor, Henri Nouwen. I hope and pray that this book will honor his life and work as a priest, writer, pastor, and friend to many. Because our paths crossed, I glimpsed dimensions of God's presence that otherwise I might never have seen. Thank you, Henri. I miss you.

I have been gifted with family, friends, and a community who have supported me through the joy and frustrations of preparing this book. Thanks to Robert Ellsberg, editor at Orbis Books, who entrusted me with this project, and to Sue Mosteller and Kathy Christie at the Henri Nouwen Literary Centre, who supplied crucial information about Henri's life and always encouraged me to tell the truth in love. I give thanks for all my Daybreak friends.

In the crucial "middle period" of the writing, my beloved daughter, Christy, accompanied me to the Nouwen archives at Yale and helped me to sort through Henri's prodigious writings. Her crackerjack intelligence, her astounding adroitness with the computer as a conceptual tool in the art of putting together an anthology, her ready wit, her love for Henri and his vision, and her friendship have been a rare and wonderful gift to this admiring and grateful father. Thank you for bringing your stalwart, compassionate husband, Bill, into my life.

Throughout this project, my wife, Margaret Bullitt-Jonas, not only encouraged and loved me, but provided invaluable editorial reviews. To my siblings, Steve and Jolene, thank you for your exuberant love of family. My beautiful mother-in-law, Sarah, offered constant, loving support, especially when my energy and vision waned. I incorporated many of her keen observations into the text.

I give thanks to the members of my writing group, Brita Gill-

Austern, Andy Canale, and Demaris Wehr, for listening with their hearts as well as their minds and for their discerning, sensitive feedback.

Thanks be to my spiritual community, The Empty Bell. Each week we sit in silence together, believing in faith that somehow the grace of God is at work in all we think, feel, say, and do. I give thanks for your love and for the fearless, adventuresome spirit in which you pray.

Finally, there is no one who inspires me, no one who reminds me more of God's hope, good-heartedness, and joy than my dear son, Sam.

Permissions

Sources

"All Is Grace," *Weavings* 7:38–41 (November–December 1992).

Behold the Beauty of the Lord: Praying with Icons (Notre Dame, Ind.: Ave Maria Press, 1987).

"Being the Beloved" (sermon), broadcast on *The Hour of Power* (Crystal Cathedral Ministries), August 23, 1992.

Beyond the Mirror: Reflections on Death and Life (New York: Crossroad, 1990).

Bread for the Journey: A Daybook of Wisdom and Faith (San Francisco: HarperSanFrancisco, 1997).

Can You Drink the Cup? (Notre Dame, Ind.: Ave Maria Press, 1996).

Clowning in Rome: Reflections on Solitude, Celibacy, Prayer, and Contemplation (Garden City, N.Y.: Doubleday, 1979).

Compassion: A Reflection on the Christian Life, with Donald P. McNeill and Douglas A. Morrison (Garden City, N.Y.: Doubleday, 1982).

Creative Ministry (Garden City, N.Y.: Doubleday, 1972).

A Cry for Mercy (New York: Doubleday, 1981; Maryknoll, N.Y.: Orbis Books, 1994).

Genesee Diary (Garden City, N.Y.: Doubleday, 1976).

¡Gracias! A Latin American Journal (San Francisco: Harper & Row, 1983; Maryknoll, N.Y.: Orbis Books, 1993).

Heart Speaks to Heart: Three Prayers to Jesus (Notre Dame, Ind.: Ave Maria Press, 1989).

Here and Now: Living in the Spirit (New York: Crossroad, 1994).

The Inner Voice of Love: A Journey through Anguish to Freedom (New York: Doubleday, 1996).

Letters to Marc about Jesus (San Francisco: Harper & Row, 1988).

Life of the Beloved: Spiritual Living in a Secular World (New York: Crossroad, 1996).

Lifesigns: Intimacy, Fecundity and Ecstasy in Christian Perspective (New York: Doubleday, 1986).

Love in a Fearful Land: A Guatemalan Story (Notre Dame, Ind.: Ave Maria Press, 1985).

Making All Things New: An Invitation to the Spiritual Life (San Francisco: HarperSanFrancisco, 1981).

Our Greatest Gift: A Meditation on Dying and Caring (San Francisco: HarperSanFrancisco, 1994).

"Parting Words: A Conversation on Prayer with Henri Nouwen," in *Sacred Journey:* The Journal of the Fellowship in Prayer, vol. 47 no. 6:8–20 (December 1996).

The Primacy of the Heart: Cuttings from a Journal, ed. Lewy Olfson (Madison, Wis.: St. Benedict Center, 1988).

Reaching Out: The Three Movements of Spiritual Life (Garden City, N.Y.: Doubleday, 1966).

The Return of the Prodigal Son: A Meditation on Fathers, Brothers, and Sons (New York: Doubleday, 1992).

The Road to Daybreak: A Spiritual Journey (New York: Doubleday, 1988).

"Spirituality and the Family," *Weavings* 3:6–12 (January–February 1988).

"A Tribute to Henri Nouwen: 1932–1996," a Windborne video production.

"The Vulnerable God," *Weavings* 8:28–35 (July–August 1993).

Walk with Jesus: Stations of the Cross (Maryknoll, N.Y.: Orbis Books, 1990).

The Way of the Heart (San Francisco: Harper & Row, 1981).

With Burning Hearts: A Meditation on the Eucharistic Life (Maryknoll, N.Y.: Orbis Books, 1994).

Introduction

The Fire of the Beloved

A white robe falls loosely over his body. Around his neck hangs a long, woven, multicolored stole from Central America. Fr. Henri Nouwen is sitting on a chair, hunched over a long wooden table. His large hands reach forward to surround the glass chalice, half-full of red wine. With wide-open eyes, he looks around the room, and then down at the prayers in a large missal propped on the white linen of the altar. From time to time, during the Eucharistic prayer, Henri closes his eyes tightly as if trying to focus all his energies. Here in his own darkness, he wants a quiet moment with Jesus. Painfully aware of his own limitations, he has come here to plead for this community of seekers.

> *Blessed are you, Lord, God of all creation. . . . By the mystery of this water and wine may we come to share in the divinity of Christ, who humbled himself to share in our humanity.*

Over the years, the clear glass chalice has reflected the faces of many thousands who have come to hear the Word: handicapped people lying across bean-bag chairs, lay care-givers, Catholic priests and Protestant ministers, Latin American peasants, professors, middle-class Catholics, wealthy philanthropists, seminary students, and United States Senators. They come to hear the Word, but also to be in the presence of the radiance that seems to stream from this man. They come because they hope to receive, into their own shadows of doubt, despair, and hopelessness, a bit of his reflected, dancing light. And perhaps to discover their own. They come because this man, more than anyone else they know, seems not only to speak the Word, but actually to *become* it. Some say that when Henri Nouwen presides at a Eucharist, one not only hears but *sees* the Word, right here, right now.

Since his death, the memories of some who heard him have no doubt faded. But for others, the memories have grown in power and significance. Emerging from the shock of Henri's death, many of us walked toward other friends who knew him. Like adolescents suddenly called into new responsibilities, we gathered in small groups, looked into each other's tear-filled eyes, and shared stories of what we'd seen and heard. Remember what he said? How he declared that we are the beloved of God? Because of him, don't we find ourselves stepping out in faith more boldly? Because of him, don't we find ourselves taking extraordinary risks to love or help others? Didn't our hearts burn in his presence? And even now, isn't he somehow here, among us?

Analogies to the life, death, and resurrection of Jesus seem both presumptuous and appropriate. Henri's friends remember clearly his ordinary human weaknesses, especially the rapacious yearnings and temptations that assailed him from his depths. We think about his many books — more than forty in all — in which he courageously stood with one foot in the shadow of self-rejection and one foot in the daylight of God's love. We know that he stood there for all of us, articulating so simply and beautifully what that wild, dangerous territory between the human and the divine looks like. Many of us would have preferred that Henri's human woundedness be less visible. But somehow, we know that his ever-present, accompanying shadow was there only because of the Light in which he walked.

•

One day, in September 1996, a package arrived addressed to our six-year-old son, Sam. Sam, a beginning reader, pronounced the name on the return address, "Henri J. M. Nouwen, Daybreak, L'Arche, Toronto, Canada." With delight, Sam tore open the brown paper package to find a shiny gold penny whistle. Henri had sent it from an airport as he traveled from his community in Toronto to his beloved home-country of Holland. How like Henri, I thought, as Sam and I passed the whistle back and forth, enjoying its bell-like tones and simple melodies. Henri loved music, loved to send gifts to his friends, loved children, and loved to travel. I looked forward to telling him how the penny whistle had brightened our day.

I knew that Henri was on his way to the Hermitage Museum in St. Petersburg, Russia, to be filmed in a documentary focusing on one of its most famous paintings, Rembrandt's *Return of the Prodigal Son*. In 1957, Henri had been ordained a Roman Catholic priest for the archdiocese of Utrecht, Holland. Then, with the permission of his Dutch bishop, he had made the world his parish for almost forty years. Over the years, he told the parable of the prodigal son to rich and poor alike, in middle-class parishes, Roman Catholic and Protestant seminaries, Latin American barrios, Washington "think tanks," evangelical churches, and in hundreds, perhaps thousands of small community gatherings all over the world. Henri was convinced that this parable was the center of gravity of Jewish and Christian Scripture, the heart of mystical teaching. He believed that the story of the prodigal son is somehow true for each one of us: even though we rebel, reject our birthright, and run off to faraway countries, our God will always welcome us back, embracing us with unconditional love. To each, to all, Henri offered the same glad message, the same good news, that you, and I, and we, are the beloved of God. "My friends," he would say, "I tell you that we are loved with a 'first love' even before we are born."

On Tuesday evening, September 17, a few days after finding the penny whistle on our doorstep, I received a call from Kathy Christie, Henri's secretary in Toronto. "I send greetings from Henri, and I have some bad news," she said. "Henri had a heart attack in Amsterdam on Sunday night, just after arriving there from Toronto. He's all right, but he's in intensive care."

I was shocked, but not surprised. Like many of his friends, I knew that he had been pushing himself too hard. Henri was supposed to meet the film crew for the Prodigal Son project in Amsterdam, and then fly with them to St. Petersburg. But after the flight from Canada, he was exhausted and lay down for a nap. Suddenly awakening with pain in his chest, he called the hotel desk and was whisked by ambulance to the intensive care unit of a small teaching hospital nearby. On Monday and Tuesday, Henri endured much pain in his chest and back. His father, brothers, and sister rushed to his bedside, and by Tuesday afternoon, his friend Nathan Ball, director of the Daybreak community in Toronto, had arrived.

Kathy added, "Right now, the doctors are saying that this was not a serious attack, but that Henri will need plenty of time to recuperate." I asked her to tell Henri that I would make arrangements to visit him in the next few days.

On Wednesday morning, I called Northwest Airlines to arrange for a flight to Holland. Feeling sad, and a little desperate, I was reassured by the pleasant voice of the ticket agent. Yes, she said, I could be in Amsterdam within twenty-four hours. As she conveyed the flight information to me, she paused, "Just a minute please. I'll need to put you on hold."

As bland music poured into my ear, I imagined Henri in airports all over the world, pulling his suitcase-on-wheels, nervously searching for his gate. Suddenly, the kind woman was back.

"I'm sorry," she offered, "but our office is really buzzing right now. We've just had an announcement that a man had a heart attack while on board one of our flights. A Northwest flight attendant did CPR and the man started breathing again. We think he'll be okay."

The woman's dramatic story seemed to create an unusual bridge between us, so I told her about my friend Henri, how he too had just suffered a heart attack. When I mentioned his being a Catholic priest and writer, she paused and said, "Hmm. He sounds familiar. How do you spell his first name?"

"Henri with an 'i,' and Nouwen, N-o-u-w-e-n," I said.

"You're kidding," she exclaimed. "I think I'm reading a book by him right now! I can't really tell, because the cover is torn off, but I've been reading these little reflections for about a year. One in particular, called 'Come to Me.' Isn't this remarkable? Yes, I remember. Isn't he the man who went to live with some unusual people?"

"The handicapped of L'Arche," I replied. "In France, and then at their Daybreak community in Toronto."

"Yes," she said. "He was a university professor, but left to work with the handicapped. Please tell him that his writings have helped me so much! I can't believe it. This little dog-eared book has been with me through a lot. It's saved my life. Will you thank him for me? Fr. Nouwen's writings have come up at our parish prayer group. Please tell him that we will put him on our prayer list."

Before hanging up, I learned that my ticket agent, Henri's anonymous friend, was Liz Solano, sitting at a desk in Detroit. But I could have been talking with any one of thousands of people, from all over America and Europe, who had been blessed by Henri's inspiring and comforting words.

Henri and I spoke by phone later in the week. Feeling assured that the doctor's diagnosis of a "slight" heart attack was accurate, Henri asked that I meet him in Toronto the following week rather than fly to Holland now. He said that he would be able to resume his normal activities within a few months.

We agreed to talk again in two days, and I hung up. Tears came easily, but I was also a little angry at the doctors for not ordering Henri to slow down. Like all Henri's close friends, I knew that his periodic collapse into physical and nervous exhaustion was caused to some extent by his frenetic, emotionally intense eighteen-hour work days. From the moment he awoke in the morning until he fell into bed at night, his mind raced ahead toward the Kingdom of Heaven, toward the question of how he could help to make that Kingdom real for himself and others, especially the poor and oppressed. As Henri lay in the hospital, hovering near death, I and many of his friends reflected on his importance in our lives.

I first heard Henri preach at Harvard University in 1983, just as I was finishing my doctorate there. He spoke about two ways to live — either in the house of fear or in the house of love. By this time I had already made a tentative decision to leave my Christian

birthright behind for Buddhist meditation. But Henri's passionate
conviction that Jesus was immediately present, here and now, and
that the house of love was real, flooded my mind and heart. I had
been born and raised Lutheran, converting to Roman Catholicism in my late twenties under the guidance of a contemplative
religious order called the Carmelites. But my Christian life had
gradually stagnated at Harvard. Henri's spiritual vision was so
inspiring, so compelling, I reexamined my lukewarm relationship
with Christianity.

I continued training in Buddhist Insight meditation, but when
Henri appeared again the following year for a public lecture at
St. Paul's Church in Harvard Square, I and a few friends hurried
there to find seats in the front row. I didn't agree with everything
Henri said, but his extravagant presence and deep faith won me
over. *What* he said was important to me, but even more fundamental was *who he was* as he said it. I watched him roam the
hall, gesturing wildly with his large hands, sometimes closing his
eyes in deep concentration, sometimes rocking forward on tiptoe
in the exhilaration of an ecstatic vision that became more and
more vivid to him, and to us, as he declared its reality.

As a graduate student in psychology, I had been trained to criticize all grand theories of reality, to seek out and to deconstruct
their unspoken assumptions, religious bias, or conceptual incon-
sistencies. But Henri invited me to another kind of knowledge, a
knowledge that valued rational thinking and critical thought, but
that also opened a door to deeper levels of understanding and
commitment. I realized that Henri was not just communicating
a body of information (with which we could agree or disagree),
but *a way of being.* Wanting to be set free from the complex web
of fear and insecurity in which I lived, and, surprised by my own
boldness, I walked up to Henri after his talk and asked him to be
my spiritual director.

Over tea the next day, we discovered many areas of common interest and decided simply to be friends. In the years that
followed, we struggled through some severe misunderstandings,
but from the start of our relationship, a deep level of mutual
vulnerability and trust was available to us. Henri accompanied

me through several major life-events in the following years —
a painful divorce, a second marriage, the birth of a son, the
death of a daughter, the founding of a retreat center, the writing
of my first book. Along with a few other friends, I accompanied Henri through the many intense changes he would undergo
after leaving Harvard in 1985 — his struggles with intimacy,
the decision to become pastor of the Daybreak community, an
encounter with depression and a nearly fatal accident in the
late 1980s, the discovery of his powers as a father-figure in his
community.

Beginning in 1993, Henri sometimes invited me along to his
lectures and retreats, to play the *shakuhachi* (a meditative, bamboo flute from Japan), and to help lead the discussions. And in
1995 Henri began his sabbatical year by living in our house from
September through December. His stay with us, in his final year
of life, was a wonderful and sometimes dizzying experience. After
breakfast with our family, he would retreat to his third-floor
apartment and write long-hand in beautiful cloth-bound journals
while a candle, given to him by his Daybreak community, burned
nearby.

The leaders of Daybreak, especially Sue Mosteller and Nathan
Ball, kept in close contact with Henri, to support and counsel
him. I had renovated a carriage house on our property in the
style of a Japanese zendo. In the mornings, Henri and I would
go there to read morning prayers or participate in the Eucharist.
I enrolled Henri in my local health club, where we went three
days a week to jog on the stationary treadmills and to swim. In
the afternoon, after a nap, Henri wrote notes and letters, made
phone calls to old and new friends, and handled publishing arrangements by phone and fax. Henri swept into my office several
times a day to send and receive faxes, and Federal Express trucks
pulled into our driveway so often I could nearly greet the drivers
by name.

With Nathan and Sue's encouragement, we tried to protect
Henri's writing time, keeping his whereabouts secret. By December, however, Henri's friends were beginning to contact him, and
he was receiving more and more visits and calls. Toward the end

of his stay, he had virtually no time to write. In the space of several months, he had re-created the very life he'd been trying to leave — long days of liturgy, pastoral counseling in person and by phone, sudden airplane trips to visit people who needed him for funerals, weddings, and death-bed consolation. I and other friends urged Henri to set some boundaries to his generosity, but he seemed incapable of saying no to those who sought his help. As a friend who had tried, for a time, to protect Henri from the exhausting demands of his important but relentless ministry, I felt helpless as I watched his anxieties and exhaustion return.

Now, nine months after Henri left our home, on Saturday morning, September 21, I was sitting on a meditation cushion receiving a lesson on the Japanese bamboo flute from *shakuhachi* master David Duncavage when my daughter, Christy, came into the room.

"There's a telephone call for you, Daddy," she said. "It's Henri's secretary."

"He's died," I said to myself. "He was bone-weary and ready to die. But it's too soon."

"Jonas, this is Kathy. I'm sorry to tell you that Henri died this morning."

His heart failed at 7:00 A.M. (1:00 A.M. EST), in the Netherlands. At first I felt no strong emotion. Somehow, in spite of my deep desire that Henri live, in spite of my earnest prayers that he be healed, I had accepted that his death was near. Of course, after his death, I would grieve more deeply, realizing that I would never see my friend again.

But in my later reflections, I realized that there was some anger in my initial lack of feeling at the news. There was a voice within me that cried out, "See what you've done? You've killed yourself with overwork!"

On another level, I thought that perhaps Henri had prepared his friends well, just as Jesus had. Most of Henri's sermons and books in the last years of his life included reflections on his imminent death. Jesus had taught Henri that life becomes fruitful only when death is faced and folded into our lives, like yeast into a loaf of bread. In his last years, Henri had gradually become transformed into a baker in God's kitchen, working the yeast of death and eternity into every dimension of his life.

Henri had repeated and lived into the words of Jesus' farewell address so often, that now, in my heart, I could not distinguish Jesus' voice from Henri's:

> *Do not let your heart be troubled. . . . In my Father's house there are many dwelling places, and now I go to prepare a place for you. . . . Believe me that now, I am in Abba and Abba is in me. . . . I will not leave you orphaned.*

Now, as I held the portable phone to my ear, I looked out into the pine trees and dogwoods in our yard. I heard Kathy say, "Early this morning he had another, massive heart attack, and before Nathan or any family members could get there, he was gone. Luckily, everyone was with him on Friday night. They said the evening Office together before Henri saw them down to the door and waved goodbye."

As we spoke, I imagined Kathy in her office adjoining Henri's study in "The Big House" at Daybreak. Henri had hired Kathy after his beloved secretary, Connie Ellis, had died of cancer. In his ten years at Daybreak, he had relied heavily on his secretaries and a bookkeeper, Margaret Sutton, to help him with the enormous amount of correspondence that flowed through his office. Each day, after his prayers, Henri would go to the office to read through many letters from friends and readers of his books. Hundreds of invitations to conferences, parishes, dioceses, interviews, and households poured in every month. Henri read every letter, responding to each one personally. Because of their sheer volume, he had to decline most of these requests, but Henri found it difficult to say no and was always overbooked. Kathy would describe Henri's office as "a whirlwind," a whirlwind rushing in through Henri's heart from a very big world. After Henri's three-month stay in our home, I knew exactly what she meant.

Nathan called me the next day. "On Thursday, Henri said to me, 'I don't think I will die, but if I do, please tell everyone that I'm grateful.' "

Growing up in Holland

After Henri's death, I learned from his family that the seeds
of Henri's tremendous energy and spiritual vision were already
evident in his childhood.

Henri J. M. Nouwen was born on January 24, 1932, in
Nijkerk, Holland, twenty-eight miles southeast of Amsterdam.
Almost immediately, it was clear that Henri was a uniquely
gregarious and anxious child. His family jokes that Henri was
restless and "on the go" even in the cradle. But Henri wondered
whether in fact he'd been anxious because he was chronically
hungry as an infant. He once told me that, before her death
in 1978, his mother (Maria Huberta Helena Ramselaar) apol-
ogized to him for raising him according to the severe regimen
of a German "Dr. Spock" who taught that the rapacious wills
of young children should be broken by restrictions of food and
physical touch.

The Nouwen family tells the story of how, even as a child,
Henri was entranced by the Eucharist. Between the ages of six
and eight, one of his favorite games was to create a small, Eucharistic setting, complete with altar, vestments, and communion
bread and water. His reluctant siblings were enlisted as chalice-
bearers and communicants. In Henri's Catholic home, images of
Jesus and Mary abounded and became the rich, inner ground of
his imaginative life. Jesus' life and word ignited powerful cen-
tripetal forces in Henri's soul, drawing every ordinary experience
into the one archetypal story of Christ. Jesus was Henri's mentor
and model of maturity.

And, right from the start, although Henri felt loved by his family, he moved uneasily in his body. He bit his nails and seemed
hungry for some kind of attention from parents and siblings that
they could neither understand nor give. Henri was convinced that
this hunger was about Jesus, and he wanted to go wherever Jesus
went. Jesus moved in the unconditional, liberating embrace of
Abba, and that is where Henri wanted to live. Now.

Henri enjoyed life, but he was always impatient, as if life itself
were sometimes an unbearable waiting for the coming reign of

God, the full embrace of his Abba. His attraction to Jesus' Last Supper is therefore not surprising. To Henri, this meal expresses the heart of Jesus' message. The divine life brings joy, opening us to love one another, but it opens us as well to the heartache of loss, the poignancy of this fleeting moment. Jesus had experienced the joy of union with God and wanted to share that joy with his friends. This extraordinary joy, he tells us, is infinite, but it is also interwoven with suffering. God's peace is available now, in this moment, but it is also interwoven with longing. All of God's life is available to each of us already, but not yet. Ordinary suffering will not be taken away, nor the suffering we must face when we bear witness to God's love and are met with the world's hostility and scorn. But our suffering will have meaning, will be lifted up, transformed by the unceasing love of God.

For decades, in almost every talk, Henri would rise up on tiptoe, stretch his arm into the air, point his forefinger toward the heavens, and declare, "We must not forget that in this life, sorrow and joy can never be separated." Rather than isolating us from each other, he would say, the lonely heartache that comes when we love others can actually draw us into deeper communion with one another, and with God. He was a master at identifying scriptural passages that promised joy in the midst of sorrow. John was always his favorite Gospel:

> You will weep and mourn, but the world will rejoice; you will have pain, but your pain will turn into joy.
>
> (John 16:20)

Facing imminent death, Jesus says of his friends,

> Now I am coming to you [Abba], and I speak these things ... so that they may have my joy made complete in themselves. (John 17:21–23)

As a child, Henri was immersed in the Roman Catholic Mass. Henri's mother delighted in sharing her love of the daily Eucharist with Henri, her eldest child. And she encouraged his call to the priesthood, the only one of her four children (three boys and one girl) to choose a religious vocation. Both his maternal grandmother and his mother prized his obvious spiritual gifts. Henri gave no sign that he felt anger or ambivalence toward either of them. To my knowledge, in all of Henri's books, correspondence, and private discussions with friends, these important women in his life appear as saints, pure and simple.

Henri attended Jesuit schools, and while in some interviews and articles he described his academic performance as a child and adolescent as "average," he showed an exceptional interest in Scripture, the Eucharist, and the struggles of his fellow communicants. During the Nazi occupation of Holland, Henri's parents did their best to maintain the familiar household routines. Henri's father, Laurent, continued his work as a trusted lawyer in the community, and his mother made her daily Mass. In the evenings, the family continued to gather to share the news of the day, their love of poetry and literature, and, increasingly, the dangers at their door. Henri remembered how Nazi soldiers came one day to take his father away, probably to the certain death of a concentration camp. He recalled the paralyzing fear that gripped the family as they stood helpless, praying that the father's hiding place in the attic would not be discovered. Fortunately, the soldiers left empty-handed. Henri once described the last year of World War II as "the horrible winter of hunger" when family members rode their bicycles into the countryside to obtain food from friendly farmers. In spite of their vulnerability, Henri's immediate family lost no members to the war. In fact, he often summarized his entire childhood as quite peaceful and protected.

Henri's uncle Anton was also a priest, ordained in 1922. Before and during the Second World War, the Roman Catholic Church still held a prominent, respectable position in Dutch culture, and Anton thoroughly enjoyed his vocation. Anton's frequent presence at the Nouwen dinner table quickened Henri's desire to be a priest. When Henri was ordained as "a naive twenty-five-year-old" (as Henri once put it) on July 21, 1957, his uncle Anton gave him a splendid Eucharistic chalice fashioned by a famous Dutch goldsmith with the diamonds of Henri's maternal grandmother. Almost forty years later, in the very month of

Henri's death, his reflections on the chalice, *Can You Drink the Cup?* were published as one of his last books.

From 1951 until 1957, Henri attended the most prominent Dutch seminary in Utrecht. Again, his interests tended more to Scripture, music, art, and the gathered community of believers than to theological scholarship. Attracted to his charismatic pastoral presence, the student body once elected him as president. After ordination, when Henri's bishop suggested that he go on to study theology, Henri countered with his own request: Could he pursue his interest in people and study psychology instead? Happily, his bishop agreed, and so from 1957 to 1966, Henri explored modern psychological understandings of the human person, first at the University of Nijmegen, and then in the United States, at the Menninger Clinic in Topeka, Kansas.

The 1960s: From Holland to America

Henri's two-year stay at the Menninger Clinic (1964–66) included some supervised counseling, study of psychology's Freudian roots and its modern derivatives from Karen Horney to Gordon Allport, and many spirited conversations with friends and fellow clinicians about the relationship between psychiatry and religion. From 1966 to 1968, as the Vietnam War intensified and America's inner cities exploded in angry protest over racial issues, Henri taught pastoral theology at Notre Dame. New academic subjects and new ways of teaching were opening up. Ever since Freud's critique of religion, most Catholic universities had stiff-armed modern psychology, labeling it secular and atheistic. Now, Henri became the first Notre Dame faculty member to teach Abnormal Psychology. And he broke new ground by bringing in Protestant psychology professors for monthly lectures.

All the while, Henri continued to serve as a priest to the academic community. He celebrated the Eucharist with students and professors, offered counseling, and began to integrate his love and knowledge of Scripture and Jesus with the realities of personal suffering, racial injustice, and world politics. His diligent work in the 1960s to help students connect the insights of modern psychology with spiritual practice and understanding resulted in many books a decade later, such as *Creative Ministry, The Wounded Healer,* and *Reaching Out,* some of which became classics in the field of pastoral counseling.

During his last semester at Notre Dame, on the evening of April 4, 1968, Henri flew to Chicago to give a lecture on religious development. On the way from O'Hare Airport to the lecture, he heard the news that Martin Luther King had been assassinated. In an unpublished essay, Henri describes the combination of shock and raw, undifferentiated emotion that ricocheted through him and through the city. When he arrived at the lecture, everyone was excited about him and his message, but, strangely enough, no one initiated questions or discussion about King's death.

> Everyone knew it but nobody wanted to know it.... We are surrounded by a war burning thousands of people alive, by prisons with unknown hatred and cruelties, by houses filled with poverty and misery. How much can we allow ourselves to know? Next morning I flew to Kansas City, surrounded by a horrifying world of artificiality.... Violence was cutting through the thresholds of restraint. Chicago and Washington were burning cities and the leaders were only concerned with one thing: law and order.... Nobody offered a way to lead these feelings into creative channels.[1]

The crises in America's cities challenged Henri to develop and express a Christ-centered vision for America. In all he wrote, all he said, Henri encouraged his listeners to keep their hearts open and to trust that the suffering that accompanies love is God's suffering, too. Henri believed that Christ continually offers a creative channel of healing, a source of energy in the struggle to bring forth, through the power of the Spirit, a world marked by justice and love.

After Kansas City, Henri flew to Topeka for yet another lecture and meetings with old friends. Everywhere he went he spoke about King's death. What would it mean for the inner cities? Would it bring together the antiwar and antiracism movements?

The next day, Henri took the midnight plane back to O'Hare Airport in Chicago. The sight of many black men and women gathering near the Atlanta ticket counter reinforced his growing desire to do something, or perhaps to *be* something. He suddenly realized that he must go to Atlanta for King's funeral. So, at two o'clock in the morning, after an exhausting three days of lectures, homilies, plane rides, and conversations in taxis, airports, and a prison, Henri caught the 2:00 A.M. red-eye flight to Atlanta.

In Atlanta, Henri took his place among the marchers, making instant friends with several mourners and feeling strangely at home in a culture that must have seemed starkly different from his white, upper-middle-class, Catholic upbringing in Holland. Here in the gathering storms of America's apparent self-destruction, Henri felt nourished by the resonant mix of grief and joy displayed by those who loved Martin Luther King and by their vision of hope. Feeling bone-tired, deeply touched and absolutely safe in this black community, he stepped out of the funeral march, dropped to the ground in the garden of Morehouse Seminary, and fell asleep.

> The long hot day had burned me and the final march broken me. But a strange satisfaction went through my body, experiencing that this was where I wanted to be, hidden, anonymous, surrounded by black people. It had been a long restless trip since that Thursday night.... And here I rested, carried along by people who kept singing and praying, and I knew that out of my exhaustion a new faith could grow, a faith that it is possible to love.[2]

In the midst of Henri's growing identification with the struggles for social liberation in this country, he had often hoped to return to his native Holland, to live, learn, and share in his own Dutch church. So, in 1968, as America reeled with the assassination of yet another prominent civil rights leader — Robert Kennedy, gunned down in June — Henri returned to Holland to teach pastoral psychology and spirituality to seminary students at the Pastoral Institute in Amsterdam and the Catholic Theological Institute in Utrecht.

Now, in his own beloved country, Henri worked toward a doctorate in theology from the University of Nijmegen and edited his Notre Dame lectures for a book on the integration of psychology and spirituality. His first book, entitled *Intimacy*, was published in 1969, and his doctorate was awarded in 1971. Soon, other books would flow from Henri's lectures and sermons — *Creative Ministry, The Wounded Healer, With Open Hands, Aging, Way of the Heart, Reaching Out,* and *Out of Solitude.* When Henri first came to the United States, he did not know that he would become a prolific writer. This vocation gradually evolved as he absorbed the realization that he enjoyed it and that people were inspired by his words. To my knowledge, Henri never experienced a serious vocational crisis or question about his identity as a Roman Catholic priest. The Eucharist would always be the ground of his personal and social identity. But the happiness and refreshment of writing emerged gradually and became an essential part of his ministry until the day he died.

And, over the years, he tried out many different kinds of writing. In the Henri Nouwen archives at Yale Divinity School in New Haven, one can find articles, sermons, and lectures that are composed in many different styles — academic and theological, clinical, psychological, ethnographic, polemical, homiletic, and literary. Like any good writer, he experiments with tone, voice, purpose, and content, and aims at different audiences.

Henri's unpublished, undated paper on the death of Martin Luther King was probably written in 1969. In it, one glimpses features of the basic style that would infuse most of his future books. Here at the beginning of his career as a writer, Henri's readers will recognize his familiar, open-hearted method of recording and sharing his own emotional responses and spiritual reflections as he walks through a community of suffering, prayerful people. Similarly, we glimpse the archetypal vision that feeds all of his writings — a conviction that, on a spiritual level, our modern world and the world of Hebrew and Christian Scriptures have a lot in common. Even now we forget that God loves us passionately. Even now we kill our prophets and try to hide our own sins and suffering. We are Pilate and the condemning crowds to one another, and even to ourselves. In the King article, Henri offers his own inner loneliness and vulnerability not as mere personal confession, but rather as a window into the human condition. He suggests that such inward, tender places can be a point of connection with all human beings, even those who seem very different from us. He ends his reflections, as always, with the message that "somehow," "somewhere" (two of Henri's favorite words for describing the mystery of God's healing presence), joy arises right here, in the midst of darkness.

The 1970s: Professor at Yale and Latin American Priest

During the period that Henri was teaching in Holland, his reputation as a writer was spreading in the U.S., among liberal and conservative Catholics alike, a wide appeal that would continue all his life. Having read a few of Henri's published articles on prayer and his new book, *Intimacy*, Colin Williams, the dean of Yale Divinity School, wrote to Henri, asking him to consider teaching at Yale. At first, Henri said no. But Williams kept up the pressure, and finally, in 1971, Henri accepted his offer of a part-time position as associate professor of pastoral theology. He moved back to North America. Henri would remain at Yale for ten years, eventually gaining tenure as a full professor.

While at Yale, Henri enjoyed the work of preparing America's future ministers for their role as Jesus' presence to a suffering world. Most of his books and seminary lectures would revolve around the themes of faith, solitude, silence, prayer, woundedness, and God's love. Even though Henri had received his doctorate in theology, he wanted, more than anything, to communicate the living presence of Christ to his listeners, both in his pastoral presence and through his writing. This interest dictated the style of composition. More and more, he dropped academic language and difficult theological terms. More and more, he directed his writing to an audience of moderately educated Christians, both Catholic and Protestant, ordinary people in the pews.

As a seminary professor at Notre Dame and Yale, Henri began

a powerful inquiry into how to heal the split between theological training and spirituality. During the Yale years, for instance, when Henri was on retreat at the Genesee Abbey, a theologian came by to give a talk on the Holy Spirit. Henri was attracted to the topic, but dissatisfied with the man's dry, pedantic manner, an approach that seemed all too familiar. He wondered, "How do you speak about the Holy Spirit in such a way that it is clear and has something to do with...concrete life experience? I had that question in 1954, and now I find myself raising it again."[3]

At Notre Dame, Yale, and later at Harvard, Henri would carry the question like a mantra, a koan, "How can one teach spirituality in a spiritual way?" He tried to bring his whole self to every lecture, small group discussion, Eucharist, and counseling session. And every student received the same message. It would never be enough to talk *about* God. He told his students that "the constant danger is that words, lectures, books, and programs about the spiritual life get in the way of the life of the Spirit."[4] The real challenge and full promise of the Gospel was to come alive, fully, even here in the classroom. Henri was convinced that seminary life should encourage each person's unique transformation in Christ.

Henri's classroom style resonated with the Eucharist, for he sought to offer spiritual food that his students would receive, digest, assimilate. He was not interested in theological debate, perhaps because he disliked direct confrontation, but also because his focus was always the immediate presence of the risen Christ, a truth which had more to do with *being* than with intellectual understanding. To be sure, each student should learn from Scripture, theology, psychology, and the creative arts. But as a community, the seminary ought to create contexts of silence and solitude, inviting students to enter into their hearts, the place of encounter with their true selves, the risen Christ, and God. For Henri, teaching and pastoring were one thing.

A Christian minister should not simply call people to "correct" theological viewpoints, to ethical discipline or dogmatic purity, although each of these may have its place. Rather, a pastor should model a spacious and nonjudgmental way of being. As he told graduating divinity school students in a sermon in 1972,

> Ministry is to convert hostility into hospitality ... the enemy into a friend. It is not an attempt to redeem people, but to offer the free space where redemption can take place. The paradox of ministry is that you are called to create emptiness, not a fearful emptiness, but a friendly emptiness where the stranger can enter and discover himself as created free ... free to sing his own song, speak his own language, dance his own dance [and] free also to leave and follow his own vocation.[5]

Henri's sojourns at the Menninger Clinic and Notre Dame were precious and intense learning experiences for him, but they also alerted him to an increasing danger in Christian ministry: the professionalization of care. As theology became divorced from pastoral concerns and as various psychological models of healing moved into the seminaries, Henri worried that Christian care-givers would begin to mistake talking *about* God for real vulnerability to God in prayer and confuse psychological "treatment" with genuine pastoral presence. His books, especially *The Wounded Healer* and *Creative Ministry*, addressed these issues, and both of them swept the pastoral counseling world by storm.

Some reviewers criticized the idea of the wounded healer, believing that Henri was calling for the removal of *all* distinctions between care-givers and those they serve. But here, Henri felt misinterpreted. He believed that Christian ministers should simply remain grounded in their own vulnerability, their brokenness in Christ, and resist the temptation to objectify their fellow Christians, making them into mere "parishioners," "clients," or "directees." To be a healing, Christ-like presence for others, care-givers must be available as whole persons who participate simultaneously as both givers and receivers.

Henri believed that certain boundaries between ministers and those they serve are good. But he was concerned about ministers who deny their own suffering and their humanity by disappearing into a professional role. Henri would develop his message to

ministers in his book *The Way of the Heart* (1983) and often
return to the issue.

In one interview, Henri pointed out that he never intended the
wounded healer to be the exclusive archetype for ministry. After
all, he said,

> Jesus played many roles: Good Shepherd, the Gate, the
> Cornerstone, the Bridegroom, the Brother, and so on. Our
> ministry should bear the marks of each of these titles.... I
> never considered the wounded healer a complete model. I
> just find that it reminds me — and maybe others like me —
> of something I was in danger of forgetting.[6]

Still later, in response to his apparent overemphasis on Jesus'
call to weakness and vulnerability, he responded,

> I am not saying it like a doormat. I am not saying I am
> nobody. I am not saying I am not worth much or psycholog-
> ically a wreck. I'm saying I am a very weak, broken, sinful,
> fragile, and short-living person — but I rejoice in it. I can
> stand under the cross of my own suffering — or of God's
> suffering — but I can stand. I don't have to fall apart. I stand
> with my head erect. I can do that.[7]

Henri enjoyed the life of the mind, always moving far outside
his own protected Catholic community for conversation, books,
and music. Although some might understandably say that Henri's
busy lifestyle was driven in part by unconscious forces, he also
maintained a hectic daily schedule because he longed to stay connected with the radical "wake up" call of the Gospel. Even in
the liberal Protestant atmosphere of Yale, he saw dangers in his
life as a seminary professor and had no desire to become isolated
in an ivory tower of comfortable *thought*. During his decade at
Yale, Henri rarely taught a full load of courses on the academic
calendar. Every year he made trips to Holland, Latin America,
and to Catholic monasteries both in the U.S. and abroad.

At Yale, Henri presided at a daily Eucharist, usually with a
small group of students and friends. Frequently, he celebrated the
Eucharist at graduations, weddings, and funerals and delivered

lectures at local parishes and pastoral conferences. He cultivated friendships with a few faculty, especially Dean Williams and his wife, Phyllis, and spiced up his teaching with seminars on Trappist monk and writer Thomas Merton and the Dutch painter Vincent Van Gogh. His classes drew Yale's brightest and most prayerful students and were always filled beyond capacity.

Accepting the position at Yale made some things clear to Henri: he wanted to write books and teach ministers, but more importantly, he wanted to make the Western Hemisphere, including Canada and Latin America, his home. Canada held a special place in his imagination, ever since his family and village were liberated by Canadian troops in 1945. It was in Canada that Henri eventually spent the last ten years of his life and finally was buried. In the 1970s, Latin America was always on his mind. Through his Notre Dame and Yale contacts, he began to make friends with priests and lay missionaries in Latin America and wondered if someday he might be called to minister to its poor. After his first year at Yale, in the summer of 1972, Henri traveled to Bolivia to study Spanish at the Maryknoll language school in Cochabamba.

In 1974, the same year that he received tenure at Yale, he took a seven-month sabbatical as a "temporary" resident with the Trappist monks at the Abbey of the Genesee in upstate New York. A daily journal of prayerful reflections and conversations with spiritual director Dom John Eudes Bamberger resulted in his best-selling book *Genesee Diary* (1976). After Henri's mother died in October 1978, he would return to the abbey for another six months, from February to August 1979. This time his reflections on daily Scripture readings resulted in his book *A Cry for Mercy* (1981).

Throughout his adult life, Henri was caught up in a cycle of long, hectic days of teaching and service, followed by periods of nervous exhaustion, depression, and insomnia. In part, his visits to the Genesee Abbey were motivated by a desire to break this cycle. He knew that the depressions limited his freedom and were an unnecessary drain on his fruitfulness, but he always assumed that the cause was somehow spiritual rather than organic or psychological. Even though he occasionally saw a secular psychologist or psychiatrist, Henri never felt comfortable with their prescriptions or suggestions. He preferred to meet his "shadow" in the protected environment of monasteries or within communities that had been marginalized by society — among the poor, racial minorities, and the handicapped. During his frequent monastic retreats, Henri would tell his friends not to contact him so that he could settle into his lifelong dream of living out Jesus' story from within the regular practice of the monastic liturgy of the hours. To some extent, his strategy worked. But often, when friends acknowledged his wishes and did not contact him, Henri took offense, as if they had abandoned and forsaken him. He both wanted, and did not want, to be alone. He wanted desperately to belong, but most often he wanted to belong to those who did not belong.

Henri's vision of a warm and regular monastic life foundered on the rocks of his predisposition to restlessness, the desire for fresh intellectual stimulation, a hunger for new friends and experiences, and a nagging, sometimes self-defeating inability to say no. All too often the friends who initially supported his periods of rest suddenly needed him for counseling, weddings, funerals, and lectures. His familiar response, "Yes, of course," was partly motivated by his desire to live his life for others, just as Jesus had done. I, and perhaps thousands of others, are thankful that Henri was so motivated. But there were probably other, more unconscious motivations as well, such as the habitual, almost neurotic need to be needed. For all of Henri's life, each of his sabbaticals and retreats would be interrupted by several quick taxi rides to bustling airports, to quiet death-bed scenes, or to rooms filled with hundreds of people who waited eagerly for a word of hope and inspiration. And Henri knew himself well. He knew that often he himself could not follow his own advice, to stay home and pray.

•

During the ten years from 1974 to 1984, Henri's published work emerges from a half dozen vibrant dimensions of his life: prayer, classroom teaching, monastic community life, pastoral work, the death of his mother, and his visits to the poor of the Latin American church. *The Genesee Diary, A Cry for Mercy,* and *Thomas Merton, a Contemplative Critic* are written in monastic settings but quickly move to the question of how to live a spiritual life outside the walls of a monastery. All speak about the integration of silent contemplation and social responsibility.

In these books and others, Henri settles into a characteristic style of writing that will continue for the rest of his life. Henri's friends joke about the fact that many of his books, and most of his sermons, are based on three points. The contents of the points may vary, but rarely the number. *Out of Solitude* is subtitled, "Three Meditations on the Christian Life," and *Reaching Out* is subtitled, "Three Movements of the Spiritual Life." I never saw Henri write out a sermon. He would arise early for morning prayer or the Eucharist, take some quiet time to reflect on the Gospel, and then jot down three "little words" that he wanted his listeners to remember.

Reaching Out also showcases another familiar "Henri-ism," framing the spiritual life as a journey from *this* to *that*, from loneliness to solitude, hostility to hospitality, illusion to prayer. This dynamism is modeled on the basic Judaeo-Christian paradigm of movement from bondage to freedom, from death to resurrection, and on Jesus' often paradoxical teachings, as in the Beatitudes, where poverty, suffering, and humility become the ground, the rich *humus,* of God's blessing.

For Jesus, and for Henri, the spiritual movements from *this* to *that* require a disciplined, poetic, and paradoxical consciousness that can hold two apparent opposites. It is not that powerlessness, darkness, and death are magically transformed into something different, into power, light, and eternal life. Rather, in the hard work of spiritual discipline we discover that power is somehow hidden *in* weakness, light *in* darkness, and resurrection *in* death. In all of Henri's books, the Christian journey is a humble return to the ground of who and what we actually are, and in that return, a discerning that we are greater, more mysterious, and more beloved than we thought. Something and someone greater than ourselves shares and mirrors exactly what we are, enlarging and blessing us infinitely.

For Henri, this enlargement of the human person cannot be achieved solely by our own efforts. Under our own steam, we cannot contain and bear the deep coincidence of opposites that we are. But they are borne within us when we give ourselves to God. For Henri, the Eucharist is the inspiration and source of all self-giving. The Eucharist carries us into and beyond ourselves so that we can give happily and gratefully even when our egos press upon us to hold back. The Eucharist, he often said, means thanksgiving, and thanksgiving means celebration. Without the Eucharist, we are preoccupied with personal survival, categorizing our experience into pleasure and pain, and doing whatever we can to extend our life-spans, to maximize pleasure. The communal eating of bread and wine is a celebration in which we realize that life and death are intertwined, that "fear and love, joy and sorrow, tears and smiles exist together. Life and death kiss each other at every moment of our existence." The Eucharist is a celebration of the kiss.[8]

•

In this introduction we cannot explore fully the powerful influence of Henri's parents on his life and writing. But we might raise a few questions that will, no doubt, be examined at greater length by others. As a psychotherapist, I am well aware of a certain branch of psychology that might reduce all of Henri's life to some unconscious conflicts with his parents. Though persuasive to some, this interpretation would be simplistic, and just as inadequate as the view that his relationship with his parents had nothing to do with his message. To me, Henri's presence and ministry obviously tapped into a spiritual power that transcends the conditioning of childhood. And yet it is also obvious to me that he carried a pattern of emotional conditioning which both animated his work and fueled his inner conflicts. A few examples may suffice to make the point.

Of all his family members, Henri felt his mother most understood and loved him. He often said that it was her devotion to the Eucharist that inspired him to become a priest. Throughout his ministry in the United States, she and Henri spoke often by phone and wrote each other many letters. Suddenly, in September 1978, while visiting him at Yale, she became sick. Returning to Holland, she discovered that she had inoperable cancer. On the sixth day of the family's bedside vigil, and after much suffering, she died on October 9. Henri shared his reflections of her passing in two small books, *In Memoriam* and *A Letter of Consolation*. Of her death, he wrote,

> It slowly dawned on me that she who had followed every decision I made, had discussed every trip I took, had read every article and book I wrote, and had considered my life as important as hers, was no longer.... Indeed, I had viewed the world through the eyes of her to whom I could tell my story.... The ever-present dialogue with her had suddenly come to an end.[9]

Henri's mother's death was physically and emotionally difficult for her. In her last days, she was sometimes ashamed of her life and afraid to die. But why should she suffer like this when she had lived such a good life, always "for others"? It is surprising that Henri, who had been trained in pastoral counseling, did not reflect more deeply on his mother's life and death. Could it be that her living "for others" was partly genuine empathy and compassion and partly a more problematic "co-dependence" in which she sometimes lost touch with herself and her own suffering, joy, vision, and power by being overly involved in the lives of others? Is it possible that he was blind to this possibility because he, unknowingly, suffered in the same way? Is it possible that his wired and overwrought daily life, while healing for others, sometimes distracted him from his own darkness, thereby postponing the day of his own self-acceptance and deep healing? Given Henri's valid reputation as a wise integrator of psychology and spirituality, his occasional selective inattention to psychological insight and emotional self-knowledge is puzzling. Reflecting on the complex questions arising from his mother's death simply brings Henri back to the cross, to the idea that somehow, somewhere, God is sharing the anguish of this death, and all deaths.

One of the hallmarks of Henri's public ministry was his friendly advice that it is better to share one's vulnerable feelings with loved ones than to be isolated and emotionally self-reliant. But *In Memoriam* and *A Letter of Consolation* both make clear that Henri sometimes felt more free to share these feelings with his readers than with his own family. For example, he writes that if he had told his mother straight-out how much he loved her and how much he relied on her, she might have become "confused, embarrassed, or even offended. Or perhaps she would have simply called me a sentimentalist."[10] Both books make clear that Henri did not feel that his parents acknowledged or appreciated his rich emotional life. But Henri does not share with the reader how he *felt* about this. One can presume that some of the experiences that his mother discounted or rejected may have been critically important to Henri, but we hear almost nothing of this.

Henri's relationship with his father is equally complex. In *A Letter of Consolation,* written to his father about his mother's death, he acknowledges his father's new efforts to reach out to him. He compliments his father on his "strong personality and powerful will" and his fierce sense of duty to his legal clients. The letter conveys beautifully the love of a son for a father. But it is also a son's plea that the father lay claim to his own spiritual life in a deeper way and reexamine his aversion to those — like Henri himself — who are suffering and emotionally vulnerable. Henri's *Letter* exemplifies the efforts of many who have come through counseling, psychotherapy, and spiritual direction with a renewed desire to make contact with their parents.

All his life, Henri wanted to share more of himself with his father, and have such self-disclosure be reciprocated. But with few exceptions, this never occurred. Henri would always feel the loneliness of the spiritual and emotional gap between his father and himself. After all, although they shared many family experiences and values, these two men could not have been more different. Henri's father prized success, competition, and power and prestige in the social world, while his son cherished a noncompetitive life in community, emotional vulnerability, and the powerlessness of poverty.

After his mother's death, Henri took his father on annual short vacations to Germany and elsewhere. They saw each other regularly, but it took Henri a long time to accept the fact that, while his father enjoyed receiving his son's attention, it was difficult for his father, in turn, to give his son the attention he sought. Henri once told me that his many books lay unread in his father's study. Although he tried over the years to win his father's attention and approval, Henri's efforts to change his father eventually dwindled and finally disappeared. Henri's published work does not directly explore his anger or any depth of suffering that may have arisen in relation to his father.

Henri was no Bible-thumping fundamentalist. His understanding of Jesus' story was nuanced and more existential than moral. But in some ways he accepted quite literally the particular biblical passages that imply that anger is sinful, through and through. Despite his years of training in Western psychology, a field of inquiry which considers anger a neutral emotion with the potential to be constructive as well as destructive, and although his own field of pastoral counseling recognizes anger as a useful "signal" emotion, alerting us to danger (real or imagined), Henri never seriously explored the possibility he might be angry with his parents or need to grieve what he did not receive from them. As a result, he never discovered what many people realize who take the journey through anger into grief: a deeper level of compassion for his parents. And for himself. To the extent that he did acknowledge unmet needs, Henri preferred to resolve them not by turning to psychotherapy, but, as in everything else, by following the guidance of Scripture, to honor father and mother, to speak well of them, and to accept them "as they are."

Were unconscious forces at work in Henri's focus on God's powerlessness? Perhaps Henri's reading of Jesus sometimes overlooked the grace that can be present in the power of personal and social visions and creativity, in the power of making things happen and getting things done. Henri tended to emphasize Jesus' powerlessness, what he *endured,* what happened *to* him, rather than what he decided and created. Is it possible that Henri's interpretation was influenced both by his Roman Catholic environment (with its emphasis on compassion for the poor) and by the ways in which his father used his personal power to distance himself from intimacy, an intimacy that Henri desperately needed?

One might speculate whether Henri's particular understanding of Christian love and forgiveness had a terrible cost, a severe, lifelong repression of the emotions (and the self) his parents deemed unacceptable. I believe that the spiritual life can never be reduced to mere psychological categories. Henri dedicated his life to that within us which is truly beyond categories, the divine source and destination of our fragile and precious being. And yet we all live at the nexus of the human and the divine, heaven and earth. These powers come together powerfully in a person like Henri, and the story can be told in many ways.

•

In 1981, Henri gave up his secure teaching position at Yale. This decision came as a surprise to some, because Henri dearly loved teaching a spirituality that integrated his complex view of the world. Throughout his Yale years, in both his lectures and his books, his first and fundamental text was the New Testament, but alongside the words of the Gospel writers he enjoyed weaving such diverse voices as the mystics Brother Lawrence, St. Thérèse of Lisieux, St. Ignatius of Loyola, and Thomas Merton, the philosophers Kierkegaard and Heidegger, various Zen Masters, the psychologists Victor Frankl and Carl Rogers, and even contemporary singer Paul Simon, whose famous line "a bridge over troubled waters" offered Henri an image of what it means to minister. It is interesting to note that references to non-Christian sources decreased in Henri's post-Yale years. More and more he relied exclusively on the Hebrew and Christian Scriptures for stories, metaphors, and messages of hope. After Yale, the sole organizing metaphors of his homilies and writings became the life of Jesus and the love that Jesus shared with Abba.

Henri was often happy at Yale. Dedicating *The Wounded*

Healer to his Yale friends Colin and Phyllis Williams reflects one important source of that happiness. Williams supported Henri enthusiastically when some other faculty complained that Henri was a popularizer and not scholarly enough to be a Yale professor. When a new dean took Williams's place, Henri began to feel even more out of place among the faculty. The new administration did not welcome Henri's work as warmly as Williams had. Henri was increasingly troubled by what he considered a chronic problem among the students, faculty, and staff of American seminaries: the lack of a cohesive, supportive spiritual community. Too few people lived out the joy of the Holy Spirit, too many were narrow in outlook, often depressed under the burdens of personal suffering, paperwork, or academic competition and cynicism. In Henri's view, many religious and seminary leaders were sleepwalking when they could be dancing!

Although Henri always preached a vision of social and economic justice, he simultaneously tried not to criticize people or institutions. Just as Henri saw no reason to battle his parents, seminaries and other religious and political institutions escaped harsh judgment. Even when he campaigned for social justice in Central America, knowing well the violent and duplicitous role of the United States in Guatemala and El Salvador, he avoided direct criticism of particular politicians and particular laws or procedures. In almost all situations of actual or potential conflict, he avoided direct confrontation, focusing instead on the positive, motivating vision of the Good News. His criticisms of authority were usually tangential, or sweetened with good humor, and only rarely did they find their way into print. For example, in 1980, he wrote,

> Many seminaries and theological institutes have become such talkative places. When I enter the common room at Yale Divinity School during coffee hour, and become engulfed in the waves of lukewarm conversation in which I willingly immerse myself, I often remember this observation by a Trappist abbot. "When a novice grows deeper in the spiritual life, he not only talks softer but even walks softer."

Meanwhile, we have solved the problem with a new, very
heavy wall-to-wall rug![11]

In the spring of 1981, after much prayer and counseling,
Henri's dissatisfaction with institutional life, his sense of adventure, and his love for the Eucharist as a profound kind of social
action, led him to leave Yale for Latin America. Grateful students and friends said goodbye, thanking him for his ministry
with them and blessing his next step into the unknown, perhaps
among the poor of Peru. That year, Henri dedicated his newest
book, *Making All Things New*, "In gratitude for ten joyful years
with students and faculty of the Yale Divinity School."

•

Throughout the 1970s, Henri considered a spiritual call to Latin
America. In this tumultuous decade, the stark contrast between
rich and poor in Latin America led many Roman Catholic theologians to a vision for the church called a "preferential option for
the poor." This view, also known as "liberation theology," made
the point that the Latin American church had sometimes colluded
with the rich to oppress the poor, and that now a great historical,
spiritual correction must be made. The church must help the poor
to articulate their presence and their needs, not only in private
prayer, but openly in their cultural and economic institutions.
Henri was attracted to the idea that Christ is sometimes more
discernible among the poor. Their lives mirror the hope, the terror, and the vulnerability of Jesus. It is there among the poor that
the Good News takes root, demonstrating that in Christ, God becomes as defenseless as the weakest and most helpless among us.
Henri wanted to go to Latin America because he thought that the
reconciling Christ often becomes most visible at the margins of
society.

In the summer of 1981, after formally giving up tenure at Yale,
Henri made a short retreat at the Genesee Abbey and then began
a six-month residency in Bolivia and Peru under the guidance of
Maryknoll missionaries. He also spent several weeks in Nicaragua. His book *¡Gracias!* describes the journey. Written as a diary,

it begins in October 1981 and ends with Henri's return to the United States in March 1982. This visit would touch him deeply, but it would also make clear to him that God was not calling him to make a permanent home in South America.

Sometimes being a priest to the poor in his village energized and inspired him. For example, soon after arriving in Peru, he suddenly felt completely safe, just as he had among the black community of Atlanta following the death of Martin Luther King. As he stood,

> looking at the busy streets of Lima, Peru, the dark open faces and the lively gestures, I felt embraced by a loving people in a way I had not known before.... Sensing the gentle spirit of forgiveness, I had the strange emotion of homecoming. "This is where I belong. This is where I must be."[12]

But several months later, Henri began to feel underutilized, unappreciated, and he struggled with depression. After much prayer and consultation, he concluded that the Latin American journey "never led me to that deep inner 'imperative' that forms the center of a true call."[13]

Still, Henri would maintain his network of friends in Latin America, often speaking out in the United States about the oppressive political and economic situation that he had experienced first hand. He returned to Latin America in 1984 at the invitation of Fr. John Vesey, a friend who had just taken over a parish for martyred priest Stanley Rother. In the resulting *Love in a Fearful Land*, Henri sees the terrible brutality of Latin American dictatorship all around him but stands firm in his conviction that armed revolution, or returning hatred for hatred, is a not a valid Christian response. Jesus' way of peace must be followed.

Henri's hope in a nonviolent evolution came to him most powerfully toward the end of his Guatemalan visit as he stood with John Vesey, celebrating the Eucharist for two thousand parishioners who had gathered to pray for Fr. Rother. If Henri Nouwen could be described as a mystic, this event was paradigmatic. Per-

haps he was a mystic of the Eucharist, and moments like this
were "true north" on his spiritual compass.

> As soon as John began the Eucharistic Prayer, the people
> started to pour out their prayers in loud voices.... As I ex-
> perienced this symphony of prayer, I felt all things human
> being gathered together around the body and blood of
> Christ and made into one great Eucharistic Prayer. All the
> people became priests and lifted up their lives together....
> Misery and delight, despair and hope, fear and love, death
> and life — all became one in this wave of prayer that finally
> flowed into the prayer that Jesus himself taught us, the Our
> Father.[14]

The 1980s: Professor at Harvard and Pastor at L'Arche

In 1982 Henri received an invitation to teach at Harvard Divinity School in Cambridge, Massachusetts. Accepting on condition
that he teach only one semester per year, he arrived in Cambridge
in late fall. He taught his first class at Harvard in the winter of
1983 and, in his customary way, invited students, faculty, and
friends to attend morning Eucharists in the carriage house where
he stayed. During his three semesters of teaching at Harvard,
Henri taught courses in spirituality, especially focusing on the
Gospel of John.

After the first semester, he decided to return to Latin America, first to Mexico, and then to Nicaragua where the Sandinistas
were engaged in a desperate fight against the U.S.-backed Con-
tras. Henri visited some American Maryknoll friends, offered the
Eucharist in many villages, and met with some Sandinista leaders,
including Tomás Borge.

The Sandinistas had said that their movement was consonant
with the vision and values of the Catholic Church, and in fact
their leadership included at least one priest. But when, during
a supper discussion at my apartment in 1984, Henri was asked
about his visit with Borge, he was skeptical: "Unfortunately,"
he replied, "I felt that Borge can be quite manipulative. He is a

charismatic speaker who can get people in the palm of his hand. He can whip a crowd into hysteria." Henri put his hand out in front of him, looked into his palm, and wiggled his fingers, to represent a manipulation dance.

"I went to Borge's office, thinking we would have a nice personal talk. But Borge had invited five photographers and journalists who proceeded to take a lot of pictures while he sat next to me, lecturing me for fifty minutes on the great relationship between church and state under the Sandinistas."

Henri threw up his hands. "Borge already knows everything, and one can't get a word in edgewise!"[15]

As he met with Borge and other Sandinista leaders, Henri occasionally pointed out apparent contradictions in their stated mission of creating a more compassionate Nicaragua. Once he told me that when speaking with a revolutionary leader there, he gently suggested that perhaps they could stop using the word "dogs" to describe the political opposition.

Nevertheless, Henri felt that the Sandinistas might succeed in their mission if only they could be left alone to do it. But the United States had no patience for such a leftist experiment so close to its borders. Economic sanctions were imposed on the small country, anti-Sandinista rebels were trained at bases in the U.S. and in neighboring Honduras, many tons of supplies and ammunition flowed to the rebels, and the CIA embarked on an expensive propaganda campaign inside Nicaragua to discredit the Sandinista government. Henri saw the terrible effects of these policies on the common people of Nicaragua, and he vowed to do everything he could to speak out for peace in the region. When he returned to his home-base in Cambridge, he embarked on a lecture tour that included private, prayerful meetings with several U.S. Senators who valued Henri's spiritual advice and perceptions.

In the late 1960s and early 1970s, Henri had spoken out against the war in Vietnam and the discrimination experienced by blacks in this country. From the mid-1970s through the mid-1980s, he lectured, attended rallies and marches, and wrote about economic and political injustice in Latin America. In all these struggles, Henri's approach was absolutely consistent. Peacemaking must be the primary focus of all political leaders, whether in or out of power. But the temptations to personal power are too intense to be overcome by our insistently self-centered egos. Therefore, the peace must be God's peace, a peace that is freely available when we turn inwardly to Jesus. Jesus is the model of the ultimate peacemaker, always pointing to Abba as the ultimate source of peace, justice, goodness, mercy, love, and creativity. In order to claim peace, we must relinquish our own private agendas and let ourselves be claimed by God. Henri did not see himself as a political strategist. But he trusted that new strategies of liberation would arise from our surrender to God.

In every struggle for human rights, Henri often spoke of two dangers. At one extreme lay the hazard of sleepy acquiescence to oppression; at the other, the "temptation of activism," in which we rebel with a hatred and pride equaling that of the oppressor. He reminded his social activist friends of

> the danger that the struggle for the full liberation of the people will be narrowed down to a "fight for rights." This type of *lucha* [Spanish for "battle"] can easily lead to a fanaticism no longer guided by the joy and peace of God's Kingdom, but by a human instinct seeking to replace one form of oppression with another.[16]

True peacemakers stand firm in the affirmation of all people, regardless of race, class, gender, or social role, and are always motivated by God's love, not their own. Henri explores this middle way between acquiescence and rage in his trilogy on Latin America, *Compassion* (1982), *¡Gracias!* (1983), and *Love in a Fearful Land* (1985). Most of all, for Henri, the struggle for justice arose out of a vision of who God is, not out of a human calculus of needs and material goods.

•

In his spring semester courses at Harvard in 1983 and 1984, Henri's lectures focused on the beloved disciple, John. Henri identified with John's mystical sensibility and his intimacy with

Jesus. In John's eyes, Jesus is the meeting place of the eternal and the mortal. For John, Jesus has no beginning and no end. When we develop a close relationship with Jesus, we too have no beginning, no end.

Henri often began his classes with a moment of silence, a reading from Scripture, and prayer. Holding the Bible out before him in front of a packed classroom, he would read,

> In the beginning was the Word, and the Word was with God, and the Word was God.... He was in the beginning with God. All things came into being through him.... The light shines in the darkness, and the darkness did not overcome it.... The true light, which enlightens everyone, was coming into the world.... And the Word became flesh and lived among us...full of grace and truth....From his fullness we have all received, grace upon grace. (John 1)

In our thirteen years of friendship, I was fortunate to attend many of Henri's sermons, lectures, and retreats. In all these years, I never heard Henri read the words in the Bible as if they were merely a text. On the contrary. When Henri declared "the light shines in the darkness," you knew it was true because at that very moment he was looking at the light. He and the beloved disciple were looking at something together, wanting us to see it, too. He was touching something, and he wanted us to touch it too. When Henri read John, he declared it as the way things *are,* and even when our minds couldn't believe it, our hearts quickened. In his charismatic presence, the atmosphere in the room often became charged with possibilities, gently bringing us into a graced, altered state of consciousness. Jesus' story was incomplete, unfinished, because we were unfinished. Were we willing to complete the incarnation with our own lives?

Only the most hard-core cynic could sit impassively through one of Henri's lectures or sermons. When he sensed from people's questions or body posture that they were holding back, he would say, "Don't listen for what you agree with or disagree with. Listen with your heart." He didn't want people to agree with his theology. He wanted us to assent to the Christ within us.

Henri's shameless declaration of Christ's living presence among us was probably an embarrassment to some of his Harvard colleagues and students who were used to the fine, dispassionate art of theological reasoning. But many of them were inexplicably drawn to his exuberant faith. His classes and evening lectures were always full to overflowing. One night at Harvard, in 1983, so many people stood in the room and outside in the hall to listen to him that Henri proposed an unusual solution: "Some of you are friends who live nearby," he announced, smiling. "But I have heard that many of you have come from great distances. Therefore, I am wondering if some of you might be willing to go home tonight, so that our visitors might have your seats? In return, I will give the same lecture tomorrow night for all of you who leave now." Several dozen went home, and happily returned the following night, to another packed house.

At Harvard, Henri continued to structure his talks with three points that fit into a spiritual movement *from* something, *to* something else. Often he worked conceptually with the same movements and points for many months, or even years, in all his public speaking, writing, and sermons. From 1983 to 1985, his listeners — seminary students, Catholic parishioners, and participants in his conferences and retreats all over the country — were invited to move from the house of fear to the house of love. In the house of love, three dimensions of spirituality come alive within us: intimacy, fecundity, and ecstasy.

"But how difficult it is to move out of fear's house!" Henri would often declare in those years, adding, "In my travels in Latin America and in this country I am becoming increasingly aware of the power of fear, and how many of us live under its domination." We are afraid of the violence in our streets and homes; we are afraid of what people think of us; we are afraid of failure, of intimacy, of God; and we are even afraid of ourselves and our desires. I myself was astounded at Henri's ability to name powerful motivations that usually moved just outside the realm of my everyday consciousness. And only now, years later, am I beginning to realize Henri's wise insight that sometimes all our thoughts and actions proceed from a hidden wellspring of fear.

But even if we didn't completely grasp Henri's profound vision of human suffering, many of us believed him when he proclaimed our liberation from fear. Many of us believed him when he announced that in the core of our being, we are loved "before we were born," just as John had said, and that therefore we can walk through the world unafraid, free to love.

•

Before Henri began his third semester of teaching at Harvard, he accepted an invitation to visit a community for handicapped people in Trosly-Breuil, France. This community, called "L'Arche" (the Ark), was founded by Jean Vanier. Vanier, whose father had been the governor-general of Canada, was a professor of philosophy before founding L'Arche in 1964. Like Henri, he grew up in a Roman Catholic family that cherished the daily Mass. A serious Christian, Vanier was deeply troubled about the fate of handicapped people in contemporary society, many of whom are exiled from mainstream culture and cared for by hired professionals. Vanier envisioned L'Arche as a home where handicapped people would be valued, contributing members of small communities. At L'Arche, those who care for the handicapped are called "assistants." The handicapped are "core members" of the community. The assistants are not professionals who work eight-hour shifts and then return to their own separate communities; instead, they live in the same home with the handicapped, sharing their lives. At L'Arche, Jesus' friendship with the outcast and marginalized is the model for community: Emmanuel, God-among-us.

During Henri's six-week stay with Jean Vanier, he realized that this man embodied Henri's vision of what Jesus does in the modern world. Rather than fighting the existing governmental or political structures, he calls those around him to form a new, small community of people committed to loving the unloved, including themselves. Even though Henri would teach another semester at Harvard in the spring of 1985, he knew this one would be his last. He did not feel at home among colleagues who, he thought, valued intellectual clarity and academic competition more than Jesus' call to bring God's healing presence to those in need. He had given academic life another try, but except for one seminar at Regis College in Toronto ten years later, he would never teach a formal course again. When Harvard's spring semester was over, he resigned.

Henri had always wondered what a Eucharistically centered community would be like, and now he had found one at L'Arche. In Jean Vanier, he discovered a friend with whom he could identify — a fellow scholar who had left the academy for a spiritually inspired life with ordinary people. Henri's 1986 book, *Lifesigns,* is based upon his Harvard lectures, but never mentions Harvard. Rather, the dedication is to Jean's mother, Madame Pauline Vanier, and Henri writes that it was Jean Vanier who first suggested the terms "intimacy," "fecundity," and "ecstasy" as essential expressions of Christian community. In August 1985, Henri returned to Trosly-Breuil for a nine-month stay, to join in community with the assistants and core members, and to write. After *Lifesigns,* all of Henri's subsequent books would draw on his life at L'Arche. The daily journal of his year in Trosly was published in 1988 as *The Road to Daybreak.*

While in Trosly, Henri received an invitation to become pastor of Daybreak, the L'Arche community in Toronto. He accepted and in August 1986 moved to the place that would be his home until his death ten years later.

At Daybreak Henri tried to enter deeply into the life of the handicapped. The leaders of the community invited him to do the hard work of an assistant in the mornings and to engage in other pastoral duties and writing in the afternoons and evenings. He valiantly accepted the challenge to be a direct-care assistant with core members such as Adam Arnett, who could not move by himself nor speak. Henri struggled to have patience with this young man who required total care, and in his later writing and lecturing he shared what he was learning from Adam about being human. In February 1987, Henri returned to Cambridge to give an evening lecture at St. Paul's Catholic Church. At least five hundred people listened to his impassioned talk on Adam, in which Henri suggested that Adam was a sign that when we focus on *being* rather than *doing,* we find the secret of God's healing presence and discover peace. Adam would continue to appear in Henri's talks for the next nine years, and, after Henri's death, his story about Adam's life and death (edited by his Daybreak colleague Sue Mosteller) would be published posthumously as *Adam: God's Beloved* (Orbis, 1997).

As pastor to Daybreak, Henri's talks and lectures expressed his ongoing interest, not in brilliant Ivy League theology, not in aggressive programs of political liberation for the poor, but rather in Jesus, and in simple people of deep faith. For Henri, childlike faith was not a "dumbing down" but rather a "second naiveté" that beautifully integrates intellect and emotion. He often began his talks by leading the group in Taizé chants designed to bring about a oneness of heart in his listeners. Working with handicapped people gave Henri a chance to do something he'd always wanted to do — to say and to sing simple words of encouragement and hope to those who suffer with loneliness, depression, low self-esteem, or political oppression.

In all his lectures and sermons, Henri wanted to convey the fact that every L'Arche core member, and every marginalized person in the world, has gifts to offer, gifts of love and gifts of wisdom. The work of L'Arche assistants is to create a living situation where these gifts can be offered and received. Soon Henri began taking core members with him on his journeys across the country. He told his listeners that his audience would soon forget his words but would always remember that he'd stood before them alongside the handicapped of his community.

•

From now on, Henri's reputation as a spiritual writer and an inspired public speaker would reach beyond the bounds of Roman Catholicism and beyond the United States. In Europe, Henri's translations were handled by Herder and Herder in Freiburg, Germany, the owners of New York's Crossroad Publishing Company. Finding it difficult to find time to write at Daybreak, Henri periodically retreated to the home of Herder editor Franz Johna and his wife, Reny, and other friends. Sensing an increased interest in Henri's work in Germany, Franz Johna worked with him to publish a collection of Henri's work around the theme of Lenten reflections. This book, entitled *Zeige Mir Den Weg,* was translated into English in 1994 by Crossroad (*Show Me the Way*).

After so many years in America, Henri thought of himself as an American writer. Though he loved his homeland, he felt sorrow for Holland's almost complete secularization after the Second World War. Since his childhood, the Dutch church had been marginalized, its hierarchy sometimes retreating into a defensive, fortress-like mentality. Holland's lack of interest in Christian spirituality in general, and his books in particular, was not lost on Henri. He wished he could make more of an impact on his home country, especially among the Dutch intelligentsia and the young.

In the last ten years of his life, Henri sensed the possibility of a spiritual renewal in Holland and in the Dutch church, and so he began to reach out a little more, accepting interviews in Dutch newspapers and television and looking for good publishers to translate his books. In 1987 he wrote *Letters to Marc about Jesus,* in which he writes to his nineteen-year-old nephew (his sister's son), about the spiritual life. Originally published as *Brieven aan Marc,* it was translated into English in 1988.

•

Two events in the late 1980s stopped Henri in his tracks. In 1988 he suffered a severe emotional collapse and spent seven months in a small Christian treatment facility in Winnipeg, Canada. In 1989, he was hit by a truck while walking along Yonge Street near Daybreak. Both experiences confronted him with basic questions of life and faith. Did he really want to live? Did he really trust that God loved him? Henri was always one to see adversity as an opportunity to deepen his ministry of writing, and both events resulted in articles, sermons, and books. The truck accident almost killed him, but as he lay in a hospital bed for three and a half weeks of recovery, he composed a collection of Lenten meditations published as *Walk with Jesus: Stations of the Cross*

(1991). A year after the accident he reflected on his near-death experience in *Beyond the Mirror: Reflections on Death and Life* (1990).

The immediate cause of Henri's emotional collapse in 1998 was the deterioration of a close friendship, as he would eventually write in his account of the events in *The Inner Voice of Love* (1996). In most of his writings, Henri was not shy about sharing his own doubts and wounds with the reader. He always assumed that others suffer similar challenges, and that if somehow, in his writings, he could find a way back to the voice of love, some readers would be inspired to come along. Writing also enabled him to clarify for himself and to appropriate his spiritual insights. In *The Inner Voice,* Henri confides just how bad it was in the winter of 1988:

> That was a time of extreme anguish, during which I wondered whether I would be able to hold on to my life. Everything came crashing down — my self-esteem, my energy to live and work, my sense of being loved, my hope for healing, my trust in God . . . everything. Here I was, a writer about the spiritual life, known as someone who loves God and gives hope to people, flat on the ground and in total darkness.[17]

Henri realized that he was expecting unconditional love from his friend, something that only God could give. Henri's readers would immediately recognize that this was not a new theme in his life. In fact, the interpersonal difficulties that led to this anguish had been brewing for some time. He had vowed to live as a celibate, a vocation and discipline of loneliness that is intended to enable the priest to share fully in the life of Jesus, who was himself probably celibate. During Henri's spiritual formation in the pre–Vatican II church, the vow of celibacy meant that one should avoid all "special friendships." If particular relationships became too important, and especially if they became tinged with eroticism, they could easily become a distraction. Giving oneself to God meant giving oneself to everyone, not to anyone in particular.

Though Henri saw some problems with the rationale for celibacy, and though he felt sympathetic to the ordination of married priests and women, when it came to his own priestly vocation, he completely subscribed to the Roman Catholic worldview. He couldn't seriously imagine being anything other than priest (though he did occasionally muse on the possibility). Nevertheless, in spite of his intellectual commitment to celibacy, he sometimes found it exceedingly painful to avoid special relationships. All his life, Henri hungered to be "special" in someone's eyes.

Henri was an enormously generous person. Not a day went by that he did not call or write friends and appreciative readers, sending a message of hope or a reminder of the person's belovedness in God. Each day, someone, somewhere, would be opening a package from him, with a book and a kind inscription. And every week, at least, he sent a bouquet of flowers for someone's birthday, wedding anniversary, or funeral. Henri had grown up in the land of flowers, surrounded by oil paintings and reproductions of the lush gardens and flowers of Cézanne and Van Gogh. He savored his mother's loving skill for flower arranging. As far as he was concerned, people should be giving each other flowers and other little gifts all the time. But when they didn't, and when he noticed that he gave more of these things than he received, he struggled not to become depressed.

All the accolades that Henri received for his books, spiritual advice, and lectures were appreciated, and Henri thrived on public attention. He also felt deeply nourished by the daily Eucharist and by daily periods of silent prayer. But in his social life, especially with close friends and family, he felt a steady yearning for more: more love, more attention, more little reminders that he was special. Henri did enjoy the gratification of seeing five hundred, a thousand, sometimes two thousand people in his audience, eager to hear his message. But more and more, he also felt an aversion to such large, popular events. Henri struggled with this ambivalence until the day he died. He lived the irony of giving large audiences a hopeful message about their freedom and ultimate belovedness in God, but then often returning to his lonely room with an unshakable sense of emptiness and forsakenness. Since he knew someone in just about every time zone, he often stayed up late talking to friends on the telephone, relaxing into their voices and stories.

Henri was a passionate man who thrived on personal, intimate contact with those he loved. Sometimes, both he and his family and friends could be overwhelmed by his needs for affection. Henri himself was often not aware of the demands for attention that he put on certain close friends. Therefore, it was a complete surprise to him when they sometimes withdrew. He struggled to bring his instinctive reactions of anger and resentment to prayer. And his prayer would sometimes be flooded with the guilt of knowing he had gone too far. He often felt guilty and ashamed of his sexual feelings, even though his theology and his counseling to married people affirmed the goodness of sexuality and its share in divinity. He had inherited a longstanding Christian suspicion of sexuality, often interpreted as "the evil desires of the flesh" in conservative circles. Most often, Henri could not help but label all his erotic urges as mere "lust." He did not like the messiness of his emotional needs. He wished that his yearnings for love, attention, and affection could be met entirely in his relationship with Jesus, and he tried to live as if that were true, even when he felt no consolation.

In 1988, emotional and interpersonal anguish inundated Henri. He could no longer carry on with his commitments. He then entered into six months of intensive daily psychotherapy and prayer away from his Daybreak community in order to find his bearings.

In Winnipeg, Henri was fortunate to find Christian therapists who supported his spiritual gifts and commitment. *The Inner Voice of Love* indicates that these "spiritual guides" encouraged Henri to be more at home in his body, and they sometimes held him in their arms. One of the insights Henri gained in Winnipeg was that he had been out of touch with his body. He counsels himself,

You have never felt completely safe in your body.... Increasingly, you have come to see your body as an enemy

that has to be conquered. But God wants you to befriend
your body.... Your body needs to be held and to hold, to
be touched and to touch.[18]

Henri's friends and family knew him as rather awkward physically, and many were gratified to hear of his desire to become
more at home in his body. Never quite grasping the logic of the
physical world, he had often been surprised that food in a refrigerator could spoil. Wasn't that the point of a refrigerator, to keep
food edible forever? All the small decisions that go into making
a sandwich could trigger his impatience, and not infrequently he
would boil something dry or burn something black while he simultaneously cooked, spoke on the phone, and took notes for
his morning lecture in another city. Driving was uncomfortable,
too. Often he drove fast or slow, but rarely at an easy, steady
pace. He was known to fly in and out of the long dirt driveway
at Daybreak at breakneck speed. When they had the driveway
paved, the Daybreak staff joked that it should be named "the
Nouwen Speedway"! Once, on his way to the airport, with only
thirty miles on the odometer, he completely wrecked a new car
by driving under a trailer truck.

At Henri's funeral, his Daybreak friend and colleague Sue
Mosteller shared another legendary story. One day, she, Henri,
and some core members were making last-minute preparations to
lead a retreat. Just before the retreat began, Henri declared he
was too busy to fly with everyone else to the meeting place the
night before. He would travel the next morning.

"When the morning was underway," said Sue, "we got a message saying that Henri would be two hours late. So we went on.
Finally, toward the end of the morning, he came in with a ban-
dage on his arm and a cut on his head. He explained, 'I was
hurrying into the airport this morning, and I suddenly realized
when I crashed through the door, it was a window!'"

Fifteen years earlier, Henri had recognized the problem. Having received an intuition of a simpler, more grounded lifestyle, he
recorded this prayerful vision:

Wherever I am, at home, in a hotel, in a train, plane, or airport, I would not feel irritated, restless, and desirous of being somewhere else or doing something else. I would know that here and now is what counts and is important because it is God himself who wants me at this time in this place.[19]

Everyone who knew him realized that Henri's cycles of ceaseless activity, followed by exhaustion and depression, were physically unhealthy. He had always had a difficult time listening to his body. He was much more interested in the life of the mind and tended to see his body as an encumbrance. He was well aware of the deep grip that the old "evils of the flesh" worldview had had on him. Reflecting on his pre–Vatican II religious training, Henri knew that few Roman Catholic saints reflected at length on the goodness of the body, its beauty and worth in the eyes of God. For Henri, Pope Pius XII (d. 1958) exemplified pre–Vatican II attitudes toward the body.

"Pius XII didn't walk into a room," Henri once told me. "He 'appeared.' Above everyone, with his arms wide. Gaunt, slim, and white, he appeared, as if he were an apparition, a ghost, as if he were the risen Christ emerged from the tomb after centuries of sleep. Not able to speak. No longer, and not yet, in his body. This was the ideal of the 1950s church. And then came John XXIII whose convocation of Vatican II opened up the church, and people got back into their bodies.

"A little bit," he added with a laugh.[20]

In the ancient Christian worldview, the struggle to bring Good News to the suffering, outcast, and oppressed may well require the sacrifice of one's body and health. This sacrifice is considered trivial in comparison to the soul's salvation. In the first few centuries after Christ's death, martyrs for the faith freely gave their bodies and lives for the good of the whole. Henri understood and respected this tradition. And very often he lived it. While Henri did sometimes speak in favor of the goodness of the body — declaring that that was the point of the incarnation! — he never produced a well thought out theology to address the role of sexuality in prayer and healthy intimacy. Perhaps this oversight stemmed from his own confusion on the matter.

But at the Winnipeg house, Henri was learning to appreciate his body, to trust the emotions and sensations that he found there. He was learning the importance of allowing himself to be physically held and to know that such holding did not have to be erotic. He was beginning to understand that he should pay some attention to diet and exercise. But how would he integrate these postmodern values and sensibilities into daily life when he returned to Daybreak and the world? Henri struggled with this question until his heart failed in 1996.

Henri benefited greatly from his time away in Winnipeg, but he also grew impatient and, in the end, left treatment against the advice of his therapists.[21] He felt grateful to them but was convinced that any further healing would come through living out his life at Daybreak. One effect of the emotional breakdown was that Henri suddenly had to face his compulsion to fill every minute with two minutes' worth of activity. When he returned to his duties as Daybreak pastor, he did find it somewhat easier to say no to the scores of requests for lectures and retreats that crossed his desk every week. Somewhat.

The 1990s: Coming Home

In the early 1990s, Henri was feeling better than he had in a long time. He was enormously productive, writing more than a book a year, traveling to L'Arche communities around the world, including those in Latin America and the Ukraine, offering retreats to Catholic and Protestant clergy and business leaders, and giving lectures and talks at innumerable conferences and parishes in Canada, the U.S., and Europe. Henri was always popular among Protestants, but his reputation blossomed dramatically after he gave a series of homilies at Southern California's Crystal Cathedral, for his friend Rev. Robert Schuller's televised *Hour of Power* in 1992, one of which is reproduced in this anthology (p. 24). In 1994, the *Weekend Sun* in Vancouver, British Columbia (Saturday, April 16), reported:

A recent survey asking 3,400 U.S. Protestant church leaders who most influenced them showed Nouwen ranked second — behind a church-growth specialist named Lyle Schaller, but ahead of Billy Graham.

About this time, Henri also responded to the pleas of friends in the Ukrainian Catholic church. A friend from Harvard, theologian Borys Gudziak, had helped to found a seminary in L'viv, Ukraine. Zenia Kushpeta, a Daybreak friend, was organizing a small L'Arche community nearby. In 1993, Henri made the first of several visits to this former Communist country in which the Catholic minority had, until recently, been brutally oppressed. Henri wrote, "We visited an orphanage for small children. . . . In little beds, beautiful small faces looked at us with such a desire for attention, love, and care that I felt like taking them all with me and starting a new L'Arche home on the spot."[22]

Henri's native restlessness and his love of people called him continually into new cultures and toward new friends. On one trip to Europe, he happened upon a circus in which the Rodleigh family of trapeze artists were performing. He was so thrilled by their athletic grace and beauty that he introduced himself, and they, in turn, sensing his deep appreciation, asked him to accompany them on a tour. On subsequent visits to Europe, Henri always tried to spend some time with the Rodleighs.

Someone once asked Henri if he had become their pastor, and he quickly replied, "Oh, no. In fact, it is they who minister to me!"

For Henri, one extraordinary spiritual metaphor emerged from the trapeze performances. Here the Rodleighs were his spiritual guides. They told him to watch closely how a trapeze artist throws herself into the air as a catcher swings toward her. Notice, they said, how the catching is accomplished solely by the catcher. The one who throws herself into space must not try to catch the catcher, but simply extend her arms and allow the catcher to grab her by the wrists. Henri felt that this image captured the essence of our relationship with God. In the spiritual journey, we must throw ourselves toward God and then trust that God will catch us. If, out of anxiety, we try to catch God or to control how God should catch us, we may fall.

Henri's sojourn with the circus expressed a change in consciousness and self-identity that he was undergoing in the early 1990s. He kept a journal about the circus and began wondering how to write about this experience in a new way. For years, his friends at Daybreak had joked that though Henri had written many books, basically he was writing the same book over and over. Henri took the joking in stride. He knew that his simple, pastoral writing style nourished many thousands of people. But he also sensed another, deeper part of himself wanting to break out of the conventions and public identity that he had created.

The arts had been an important part of Henri's upbringing, and now he wondered how to bring more artistic expression to both his spiritual and public lives. He deepened his friendship with artists such as English documentary filmmaker Bart Gavignon, New York City pianist Lorin Hollander, children's TV star Mister Rogers, and Newburyport painter Steve Hawley. He became involved with a group of Christian artists who were starting a new magazine called *Image,* and in 1993 he published an article in *Image* about a new sculptor friend, Steve Jenkinson. This article is unusual for Henri because in it he uses almost no "God language." Throughout, he focuses on Steve and his work, with a minimum of spiritual interpretation, as if to convey the message that true creativity is intrinsically sacred.[23] With friends in Canada, and in California and New York, he welcomed opportunities to attend concerts, art shows, and plays, and his reading list always included biographies of painters and musicians. At the time of his death, Henri had engaged a new editor to work with him on the circus material, an editor who supported Henri's intention to move into new directions with his writing. In early 1992, Henri said,

> My consciousness has been expanded in some way. I'm not anxious about it, but it's a new world and it can be frightening. I realize how judgmental I've been, like "I'm Catholic and you're not, but should be," [he laughs], or "I'm white

and you're not," or "I'm a male and you're not." All those divisions and boundaries are coming down. Then too there's the whole question of who God and Jesus are — that is all open now. I don't think that I've been consciously judgmental. I've always been tolerant, but there's a new openness and identity with humanity.[24]

This new openness extended into non-Christian spirituality. In 1989, Henri visited the Hindu meditation master Eknath Easwaran in California. Easwaran's teachings made a deep impression on Henri. Though he did not wish to make the Hindu path his own, Henri saw much common territory between it and the Christian contemplative tradition. He took some of Easwaran's suggestions to heart in his own prayer life, and in 1991 Henri happily endorsed Easwaran's new edition of *Meditation*.[25] Henri's interest in the East was not entirely new. In the early 1970s, he had marched alongside some Buddhist monks in anti–Vietnam War protests, and he always enjoyed reading and quoting from stories of Zen enlightenment. Of course, for Henri, Jesus would always be the primary teacher. But now Henri felt a little more open to receiving guidance and wisdom from Hindu and Buddhist sources. In *Here and Now*, he speaks about the holy faces that grace the hidden boundaries of his soul: Jesus and Mary, Thérèse of Lisieux, and Charles de Foucauld, but also Ramakrishna and the Dalai Lama.[26] Henri saw his own openness to the spiritual gifts of other religions as entirely consistent with the Vatican II vision that God's grace is not contained by the Christian churches. The Holy Spirit, after all, "blows where it will." Of course, Henri's moving outside the circle of Christian spirituality did trouble some fundamentalist Christians. But his message about Jesus was so clear, powerful, and grounded in the New Testament that they could easily forgive what they considered to be his occasional lapses of judgment.

Virtually all of Henri's writings in the 1990s revolve around the central themes of belovedness, brokenness, death, and resurrection. For Henri, the core of Jesus' story is this: At his baptism, Jesus is addressed by the Holy Spirit as God's beloved Son. He is then divinely inspired to go out and share this belovedness with everyone. In living out his blessing in a fallen world, Jesus meets with resistance and rejection, undergoing great suffering. In the finality and brokenness of death, he is somehow resurrected and transfigured. His risen life becomes an eternal bridge across the divide between life and death. Through the power of the Spirit, Christ's life of compassion, suffering, and resurrection is alive in each one of us. Jesus' story is our story, and Christ is our true self.

Henri summarizes the dynamic stages of the Christ story in his important book *Life of the Beloved,* emphasizing the temptation with which he struggled all his life, the "dark voices" of self-reproach, self-rejection. Henri was convinced that all of us must contend with noisy or subtle inner voices that tell us we're not good enough, not smart enough, not attractive enough, not spiritual enough, not worthy of love.

"Over the years," he concludes, "I have come to realize that the greatest trap in our life is not success, popularity, or power, but self-rejection."[27] Many millions of people never escape this trap. But in Henri's vision, there is a way out, the way of the beloved Jesus.

In *Life of the Beloved,* this spiritual liberation expresses itself in the four distinct movements of the Eucharist: "chosen, blessed, broken, given," a theme which he continues to explore in *With Burning Hearts: A Meditation on the Eucharistic Life.* As Henri sees it, each of us is *chosen* by God as the beloved before we were born. Each of us is *blessed,* through Christ, to be a son or daughter of God. Each of us is *broken* and humbled in our relationships, work, and spiritual and political lives. And each of us is *given* by God to others, given to share our lives with others, to bless others as we have been blessed. Henri did not intend merely to present a coherent theological worldview. He intended to describe an actual experience that Christians, across the centuries, have known. In all four of its graced dimensions, the Eucharist becomes a way to live. We must continually, consciously claim that experience in order for it to be made real. Even brokenness such as self-rejection must be acknowledged and claimed as our own. If we can do this, we will know that no matter how difficult life becomes, however real the shadow of danger and death, we *are* the beloved. What's more, our lives *become* the Eucharist, as we ourselves become bread and wine, body and blood, spiritual sustenance for others.

•

In the last five years of his life, the most frequent theme in Henri's writing is death. His own death, the death of Jesus, our death. Death is not something to fear or to avoid. It is, rather, a continuation and the fulfillment of life. As Scripture says, if we live with Christ and die with Christ, then we shall be raised with him (Rom. 6:4; 2 Cor. 4:14; Col. 2:12). It is not that Henri suddenly discovered death in the truck accident of 1989. All along, he had spoken and written about death, its inevitability and its promise. Before the accident, he had already experienced and deeply reflected on the deaths of his mother and his priest-uncle, as well as those of Thomas Merton, Martin Luther King, and many friends. He had celebrated the Eucharist at hundreds of funerals, calling attention to the underlying spiritual connection between one person's death and the death of Jesus. All along, Henri had preached the simultaneity of suffering and grace in death. All along, he had shared his excitement about John's vision of eternal life, especially clear in Jesus' farewell to his friends:

> Truly, truly, I say to you, unless a grain of wheat falls into the earth and dies, it remains alone; but if it dies, it bears much fruit. (John 12:24)

> I am going to him who sent me, [and] it is to your advantage that I go away. Unless I go, the Spirit cannot come.
> (John 16:7)

For years, Henri had spoken of death as the final homecoming. Beginning with an Advent sermon at Yale in 1971 and well into the mid-1980s, Henri often repeated a story that he'd heard in Europe. During World War II, a German P.O.W. languished in Siberia's death camps. By the war's end, he was emaciated, hopelessly depressed, and near death. He questioned the value of life. Suddenly, one day, he received a brief letter from his wife. To his astonishment, he realized that she was still alive! His spirit revived, and once again he wanted to live. We are like this, Henri would say with his characteristic certainty and enthusiasm. God has sent us a letter, telling us that he is real and preparing a wonderful place for us when, at our deaths, we come home.

Henri had modeled his life on that of Jesus. Like Jesus, Henri prepared his listeners for his death by offering stories, parables, analogies. His 1992 best-seller *The Return of the Prodigal Son* explores his favorite allegory of "coming home." And his two 1994 books, *Here and Now* and *Our Greatest Gift,* offer many vignettes about the promise of death in Christ. In *Our Greatest Gift,* death is not only benign, it is something superlative, a possibility for liberation. The imminent approach of death becomes an opportunity for freedom, not only for us, but also for those we love. If we die into God's love, we set our friends free from worry, melancholy, or guilt. It is as if we tell our friends, "I'm happy. I'm fully reconciled with you and with God. I'm free to die and you are free to live. Alleluia!"

Henri refers to such an attitude as "fruitfulness." He was fond of saying that God calls us to be fruitful, not productive. To be productive is to accomplish many things through our own efforts, and of course there is a place for productivity. But to be fruitful is to receive and then to pass on God's presence, God's infinite love and mercy. When we are fruitful, we feel grateful and are happy in a way that is independent of our successes and failures, independent of our mood swings. It is not that we think about being fruitful, we simply *are.* People around us are healed into new dimensions of vitality and creativity. In the last few years of his life, Henri was consciously preparing the ground of his life so that his death could bear fruit.

Perhaps the friendly joke that Henri was always writing the same book over and over is true. From the very beginning of his ministry in America, he asked us to trust Jesus' guidance about death. From the very beginning, he counseled us to see dying as a continual process — not a sudden interruption, but a dynamic dimension of living in each moment. We should not be surprised when suffering and death come. Early in his ministry on American soil, in 1968, Henri preached a funeral homily entitled, "On Departure":

> Jesus' farewell today is an invitation to understand our life as a constant departure from the familiar to the real, a growing sense of freedom and independence,...a constant dying away from the past in which the final departure is a final independence. Life is a school in which we are trained to depart. If this is true, death is no longer a cruel destiny [that] ruins all efforts..., but a signal to deeper understanding. We can love, not in spite of death, but because of it. We cannot love immortal things. Only what is irreplaceable, unique, and mortal can touch our deepest human sensitivities and be a source of hope and consolation. God became lovable only when he became mortal. He became our Savior because his mortality was not fatal but *the way* to hope.[28]

Henri wanted everyone to know that when we fully claim who we really are, our living and our dying, God will bear fruit in us. Instead of worrying about what to do, we should turn to God in prayer. God's Spirit will guide us, and the most fruitful course of "doing" will follow. The fruitfulness will belong to God, not to ourselves.

One of Henri's last books, *Can You Drink the Cup?* was published in the month he died. To drink the cup is to accept and befriend the totality of who we are. As with many of Henri's favorite scriptural images, he had used the metaphor of the cup before. In a 1967 sermon he tells us that a priest cannot be helpful to others unless he himself "really lives and drinks the cup of life to the bottom."[29] For him, drinking from the Eucharistic cup had always been a courageous act, an expression of our willingness to cast off any sense of victimhood and accept completely our one unique life.

Henri did not wait until he was perfect before beginning his ministry, before proclaiming the Good News to others. Even at the time of his death, when he had reached a deeper level of trust in God, he was still a wounded healer. In a 1994 interview, he confessed, "I need an enormous amount of friendship and love to be well. I'm extremely vulnerable, extremely needy. On the other hand, I think I give a lot."[30] In 1994, in Houston, Henri happily received a St. Martin de Porres Award for his Christian ministry. At that ceremony, he offered this spiritual self-assessment: "Don't romanticize me. It's not that I did something dramatic," he said. "In fact, I'm still competitive. I'm still ambitious. I'm still in turmoil a lot — but in community with people who keep calling me back to the truth."[31]

Henri's inner struggles were visible in all his writing, and his hope was that in acknowledging his weakness and vulnerability he would give his readers permission to claim our own "shadow side" and to see that Christ is present even there — and, perhaps, especially there. The success of Henri's books and the enthusiasm with which his many public appearances were received indicate that his hope was often fulfilled.

·

Throughout his public life, Henri counseled his fellow Christian leaders to beware of the same three temptations that assaulted Jesus: the temptations to be relevant, to be spectacular, and to be powerful. It is ironic, and illustrative of the paradoxical nature of Henri's ministry, that in choosing the way of a priest, the way of "downward mobility," he ended his life being seen by many as extremely relevant, quite spectacular, and a powerful spiritual presence on this earth. At the same time, his relevance and his power were indeed often invisible in terms of immediate economic or political significance, and his ministry — to my knowledge — produced no miraculous cures. And even though Henri occasionally longed to see one of his books favorably reviewed in the *New York Times Review of Books* (there never was a review), he was comfortable with the impact of his work. Knowing that not everyone in first-century Judea appreciated Jesus' spiritual authority and mission, he felt that he was in good company.

Jesus' farewell meal to his friends was Henri's spiritual center of gravity. He always wanted to go out from, and return to, the table of communion with his friends, just as Jesus had. Henri celebrated the Eucharist every day, but too often he did it alone or with people with whom he could not share his most intimate struggles. He could quickly become exhausted and depressed. When, through his own courage and by God's grace, he was able to connect again with community, once again he would become lit from within by a fire that perhaps only a few are privileged to experience.

Henri made a life among the poor, but his success in teaching and writing also made his name a household word for millions of spiritual seekers. In the last decade of his life, he often traveled with a handicapped person from his community. But just as often, his travels brought him to the homes and institutions of the wealthy and powerful. His words and message were simple, and he chose to write in simple prose, but people with great power in the secular and religious worlds sought his advice: America's First Lady, Hillary Rodham Clinton, once said that Henri's *Return of the Prodigal Son* topped her list of spiritual reading, and Chicago's Cardinal Joseph Bernardin gratefully received Henri's spiritual guidance as he prepared for his death.[32] Henri was a much sought after spiritual director among the handicapped and the able-bodied assistants of L'Arche and also among some of the politically and financially powerful of North America.

For Henri, the communal meal was open to all, women, men and children, rich and poor, marginalized and successful. Henri saw every person as a child of God, whether baptized or not. But he also counseled non-Christians that the full meaning and value of the Eucharist would be revealed only if they chose to be baptized. If that baptism was in the Roman Catholic Church, so much the better. In his years at Daybreak, he happily offered spiritual preparation for baptism and for entrance into the Roman Catholic Church. The handicapped of L'Arche were his chalice-bearers, sometimes offering him the bread and wine of Jesus' presence both in the Eucharist and in daily life.

For most of his adult life, Henri's ministry had been a solo expedition. He had grown accustomed to going out alone into the world. But at Daybreak, he felt that he had found his home, and he gradually integrated his ministry with that of the staff and his fellow residents. He even joined a men's group with a few other staff to explore deeper levels of friendship and mutual support. Henri never thought that the holy table — the symbol of our fundamental human unity — was something we must "try" to create from nothing. He considered our unity in God, as a family in God, a fundamental birthright that is always, already, here. As he wrote in *Clowning in Rome,*

> In solitude we become aware that we were together before we came together and that community life is not a creation of our will but an obedient response to the reality of our being united.[33]

Henri pointed to Jesus as the personal manifestation of a hidden, loving God, and to the Eucharist as the ultimate communal experience of God's presence. Many of us grew to appreciate these spiritual realities more deeply through him. But it was not just the Eucharist or even Jesus that we came to love in Henri's pastoring. We also came to love Henri himself. Perhaps this powerful and frail, healed and broken, happy and sorrowful man embodied something to which the Eucharist points. For those who believe Henri's vision, this meal that he loved is a tuning of heaven and earth, a true alignment and integration of mortal and immortal, temporal and eternal.

Every day of his life, in every situation, Henri lifted his eyes and heart toward Jesus and the Eucharist. His perseverance did not save him from personal suffering, cure his emotional wounds, make him an effective agent of social change, or answer everybody's spiritual questions. But perhaps the tangible results of Henri's faithfulness and constancy of vision illustrate the ancient Christian aphorism that "we become what we love." Perhaps, because he loved the Eucharist so completely, his life and death are gradually becoming sacred bread and wine for others.

Henri Nouwen remained a complex person to the end, but it is also true that in his final years many friends felt graced to see him grow in self-acceptance and inner peace — the fruit of his lifelong intention to receive God's love fully. He showed us all that the very things we often flee — our vulnerability and mortality — can, at any moment, become the place of holy transfiguration, for us and for our world.

Notes

1. Henri J. M. Nouwen, "The Death of Martin Luther King," Yale Divinity School Archives, unpublished paper, no date [probably 1969].

2. Ibid.

3. Henri J. M. Nouwen, *The Genesee Diary: Report from a Trappist Monastery* (New York: Doubleday, 1976), 150.

4. Henri J. M. Nouwen, from his class notes for "Introduction to the Spiritual Life" at Harvard Divinity School, Spring 1985, Yale Divinity School archives.

5. Henri J. M. Nouwen, Sermon: "Ministry as Hospitality," June 11, 1972 (based on readings Genesis 18:1–10 and Luke 24:13–35), 3.

6. Henri J. M. Nouwen, response within article by John Robert McFarland, "The Minister as Narrator" (review of "the wounded healer" idea), *Christian Ministry* (January 1987): 19–21.

7. Henri J. M. Nouwen, "For Henri Nouwen, Death Not So Mortal," interview with NCR editor Tom Fox, *National Catholic Reporter,* April 1, 1994.

8. Henri J. M. Nouwen, *Creative Ministry: Beyond Professionalism in Teaching, Preaching, Counseling, Organizing, and Celebrating* (New York: Doubleday, 1971), 91.

9. Henri J. M. Nouwen, *In Memoriam* (Notre Dame, Ind.: Ave Maria Press, 1980, 1984), 56.

10. Ibid., 35.

11. Henri J. M. Nouwen, "Silence, the Portable Cell: The Word Which Creates Communion," part 2 of a series, *Sojourners* (July 1980): 24.

12. Henri J. M. Nouwen, *¡Gracias! A Latin American Journal* (Maryknoll, N.Y.: Orbis Books, 1996; Harper & Row, 1983, 1993), 3.

13. Ibid., x.

14. Henri J. M. Nouwen, *Love in a Fearful Land: A Guatemalan Story* (Notre Dame, Ind.: Ave Maria Press, 1985), 95–96.

15. Personal communication with the editor, summer 1984.

16. *¡Gracias!* 138.

17. Henri J. M. Nouwen, *The Inner Voice of Love: A Journey through Anguish to Freedom* (New York: Bantam, 1996), xiii.

18. Ibid., 19.

19. Nouwen, *Genesee Diary,* 60.

20. Henri J. M. Nouwen, personal conversation with the editor.

21. Personal communication with the editor.

22. Henri J. M. Nouwen, "Henri J. M. Nouwen: Pilgrimage to the Christian East," *New Oxford Review* (April 1994): 11–17.

23. Henri J. M. Nouwen, "Touching Stone: The Sculpture of Steve Jenkinson," *Image: A Journal of the Arts and Religion* no. 4 (Fall 1993): 14–22.

24. Personal conversation with the editor.

25. Eknath Easwaran, *Meditation: A Simple Eight-Point Program for Translating Spiritual Ideas into Daily Life* (Tomales, Calif.: Nilgiri Press, 1978, 1991).

26. Henri J. M. Nouwen, *Here and Now: Living in the Spirit* (New York: Crossroad, 1994), 95.

27. Henri J. M. Nouwen, *Life of the Beloved: Spiritual Living in a Secular World* (New York: Crossroad, 1992), 27.

28. Henri J. M. Nouwen, draft of a sermon, May 12, 1968, in Yale Divinity School Archives of Henri Nouwen's work.

29. Henri J. M. Nouwen, draft of a sermon, April 24, 1967, in Yale Divinity School Archives of Henri Nouwen's work.

30. Henri J. M. Nouwen, interview in the *Weekend Sun* (Vancouver, B.C.), Saturday, April 16, 1994.

31. Reported in the *Times Union* of Albany, N.Y., Saturday, May 28, 1994, B-8. The St. Martin de Porres Award is offered by the Southern Dominicans, a Roman Catholic religious order. The other honoree was Patti Ruth Linbeck, recognized for her work with Right to Life.

32. Personal communication, May 1996. See also Kenneth L. Woodward and John McCormick, "For the Journey Everyone Must Face, Cardinal Joseph Bernardin Illuminated the Trail," Lifestyle section, *Newsweek Magazine,* November 25, 1996.

33. *Clowning in Rome: Reflections on Solitude, Celibacy, Prayer, and Contemplation* (New York: Doubleday, Image Books, 1979), 14.

HENRI
NOUWEN

Selected Writings

Henri trusted completely in Jesus and the transforming power of the Gospel. He entrusted his life, with stunning fervor, to the idea that Jesus was a complete manifestation of God as both mystery and unconditional love. And yet, Henri's ministry was based on the conviction that Jesus' story is somehow our story also. Somewhere, within the life of Jesus, we could discover not merely facts about a holy man who lived two thousand years ago, but secrets of our own true selves.

When Henri searched the Scriptures for clues about our real identity as children of God, he often returned to certain key passages. The following selected excerpts from Henri's writings flow from one such passage in the Gospel of Luke.

Now during those days Jesus went out to the mountain to pray; and he spent the night in prayer to God. And *when day came, he called his disciples and chose twelve of them.... He came down with them and stood on a level place, with a great crowd of his disciples and a great multitude of people.... They had come to hear him and to be healed of their diseases; and those who were troubled with unclean spirits were cured. And all in the crowd were trying to touch him, for power came out from him and healed all of them. (Luke 6:12–19)*

For Henri, every Christian's journey moves with Jesus through invariable dimensions, from silence, solitude, and prayer to community to ministry. While these stages proceed chronologically, they also fold into one another as simultaneous dimensions of our being in God. Finding an infinite, lonely yearning for God in our hearts, we go to a quiet place of prayer. There, we offer ourselves to God and receive the blessing of belovedness. God says, "You are my beloved son, you are my beloved daughter." As we receive the blessing in solitude and silent prayer, we are led back down the mountain, into a suffering world where so many people do not experience their belovedness.

The following selections from Henri's works follow this paradigmatic scheme of Luke's story as we move through the various sections from our conversion in solitude to community formation and then to the ministry of bringing Good News to the wider world beyond our own small communities.

1

The Christian Path

❊

This first section introduces Henri's overall vision of the spiritual life, focusing especially on the activity of prayer. While prayer and the personal experience of divine reality can take many forms — some of which Henri outlines in the passages presented — all of them are rooted in solitude and silence.

THE SPIRITUAL LIFE

Spiritual Transformation

In his priestly prayer, [Jesus] leaves no doubt about his intentions:

> Father, may they be one in us, as you are in me and I am in you....I have given them the glory you gave to me, that they may be one as we are one. With me in them and you in me, may they be so completely one that the world will realize...that I have loved them as much as you loved me...(John 17:21–26).

These words beautifully express the nature of Jesus' ministry. He became like us so that we might become like him. He did not cling to his equality with God, but emptied himself and became as we are so that we might become like him and thus share in his divine life.

This radical transformation of our lives is the work of the Holy Spirit.

3

... "Being in the world without being of the world." These
words summarize well the way Jesus speaks of the spiritual life. It
is a life in which we are totally transformed by the Spirit of love.
Yet it is a life in which everything seems to remain the same. To
live a spiritual life does not mean that we must leave our families, give up our jobs, or change our ways of working; it does not
mean that we have to withdraw from social or political activities,
or lose interest in literature and art; it does not require severe
forms of asceticism or long hours of prayer.... What is new is
that we have moved from the many things to the Kingdom of
God. What is new is that we are set free from the compulsions
of our world and have set our hearts on the only necessary thing.
What is new is that we no longer experience the many things,
people, and events as endless causes for worry, but begin to experience them as the rich variety of ways in which God makes his
presence known to us.   — *Making All Things New,* 52–58

Leaving Father and Mother

For most of my life I have given a quite literal interpretation to
Jesus' words: "Leave your father, mother, brothers and sisters for
the sake of my name." I thought about these words as a call to
move away from one's family, get married, enter a monastery or
convent, or go to a faraway country to do missionary work. Although I still feel encouraged and inspired by those who make
such a move for the sake of Jesus' name, I am discovering, as
I grow older, that there is a deeper meaning to this "leaving."
Lately I have become aware of how much our emotional life is
influenced by our relationship with our parents, brothers, and sisters. Quite often this influence is so strong that, even as adults
who left our parents long ago, we remain emotionally bound
to them. Only recently, I realized that I still wanted to change
my father, hoping that he would give me the kind of affection I
desired....

In this context, Jesus' call to leave father and mother, brothers, and sisters, receives a whole new meaning. Are we able and

willing to unhook ourselves from the restraining emotional bonds that prevent us from following our deepest vocation? ...

Leaving father, mother, brothers, and sisters for Jesus' sake is a lifelong task. It is only gradually that we realize how we go on clinging to the negative as well as to the positive experiences of our youth and how hard it is to leave it all and be on our own. To leave "home," whether it was a good or a bad home, is one of the greatest spiritual challenges of our life.

—*Here and Now,* 112–13

Coming Home to the First Love

Words for "home" are often used in the Old and New Testaments. The Psalms are filled with a yearning to dwell in the house of God, to take refuge under God's wings, and to find protection in God's holy temple; they praise God's holy place, God's wonderful tent, God's firm refuge. We might even say that "to dwell in God's house" summarizes all the aspirations expressed in these inspired prayers. It is therefore highly significant that St. John describes Jesus as the Word of God pitching his tent among us (John 1:14). He not only tells us that Jesus invites him and his brother Andrew to stay in his home (John 1:38, 39), but he also shows how Jesus gradually reveals that he himself is the new temple (John 2:19) and the new refuge (Matt. 11:28). This is most fully expressed in the farewell address, where Jesus reveals himself as the new home: "Make your home in me, as I make mine in you" (John 15:4).

Jesus, in whom the fullness of God dwells, has become our home. By making his home in us he allows us to make our home in him. By entering into the intimacy of our innermost self he offers us the opportunity to enter into his own intimacy with God. By choosing us as his preferred dwelling place he invites us to choose him as our preferred dwelling place. This is the mystery of the incarnation.

Here we come to see what discipline in the spiritual life means. It means a gradual process of coming home to where we belong and listening there to the voice which desires our attention.

It is the voice of the "first love." St. John writes: "We are to love...because God loved us first" (1 John 4:19). It is this first love which offers us the intimate place where we can dwell in safety. The first love says: "You are loved long before other people can love you or you can love others. You are accepted long before you can accept others or receive their acceptance. You are safe long before you can offer or receive safety." Home is the place where that first love dwells and speaks gently to us. ...Prayer is the most concrete way to make our home in God.

— Lifesigns, 37, 39

From the House of Fear to the House of Love

How can we live in the midst of a world marked by fear, hatred, and violence, and not be destroyed by it? When Jesus prays to his Father for his disciples he responds to this question by saying, "I am not asking you to remove them from the world but to protect them from the evil one. They do not belong to the world any more than I belong to the world" (John 17:15–16).

To live in the world without belonging to the world summarizes the essence of the spiritual life. The spiritual life keeps us aware that our true house is not the house of fear, in which the powers of hatred and violence rule, but the house of love, where God resides.

Hardly a day passes in our lives without our experience of inner or outer fears, anxieties, apprehensions, and preoccupations. These dark powers have pervaded every part of our world to such a degree that we can never fully escape them. Still it is possible not to belong to these powers, not to build our dwelling place among them, but to choose the house of love as our home. This choice is made not just once and for all but by living a spiritual life, praying at all times, and thus breathing God's breath. Through the spiritual life we gradually move from the house of fear to the house of love.

— Behold the Beauty of the Lord, 19–20

Listening: A Spiritual Discipline

"How hard it is," Jesus exclaims, "...to enter the Kingdom of God" (Mark 10:23). And to convince us of the need for hard work, he says, "If anyone wants to be a follower of mine, let him renounce himself and take up his cross and follow me" (Matt. 16:24).

Here we touch the question of discipline in the spiritual life. A spiritual life without discipline is impossible. Discipline is the other side of discipleship. The practice of a spiritual discipline makes us more sensitive to the small, gentle voice of God. The prophet Elijah did not encounter God in the mighty wind or in the earthquake or in the fire, but in the small voice (see 1 Kings 19:9–13). Through the practice of a spiritual discipline we become attentive to that small voice and willing to respond when we hear it.

From all that I said about our worried, overfilled lives, it is clear that we are usually surrounded by so much inner and outer noise that it is hard to truly hear our God when he is speaking to us. We have often become deaf, unable to know when God calls us and unable to understand in which direction he calls us. Thus our lives have become absurd. In the word "absurd" we find the Latin word *surdus,* which means "deaf." A spiritual life requires discipline because we need to learn to listen to God, who constantly speaks but whom we seldom hear. When, however, we learn to listen, our lives become obedient lives. The word "obedient" comes from the Latin word *audire,* which means "listening." A spiritual discipline is necessary in order to move slowly from an absurd to an obedient life, from a life filled with noisy worries to a life in which there is some free inner space where we can listen to our God and follow his guidance. Jesus' life was a life of obedience. He was always listening to the Father, always attentive to his voice, always alert for his directions. Jesus was "all ear." That is true prayer: being all ear for God. The core of all prayer is indeed listening, obediently standing in the presence of God....

— *Making All Things New,* 66–68

Enough Light for the Next Step

Often we want to be able to see into the future. We say, "How will next year be for me? Where will I be five or ten years from now!" There are no answers to these questions. Mostly we have just enough light to see the next step: what we have to do in the coming hour or the following day. The art of living is to enjoy what we can see and not complain about what remains in the dark. When we are able to take the next step with the trust that we will have enough light for the step that follows, we can walk through life with joy and be surprised at how far we go. Let's rejoice in the little light we carry and not ask for the great beam that would take all shadows away.

— *Bread for the Journey,* January 8

PRAYER

A Symphony of Prayer (in Guatemala)

All indeed is prayer. But only through a deeply committed ministry can this statement become true for us....

All of this became most visible during the Sunday afternoon Eucharist in the church of Santiago. John [Fr. John Vesey] stood behind the altar in a white alb and a brilliant colored stole made by the people of the town. Before him more than two thousand women, men, and children, dressed in the rich colors of the Tzutuhil people, had gathered to pray. As soon as John began the Eucharistic Prayer, the people started to pour out their prayers in loud voices. Everyone expressed their own fears and hopes, asked their own favors, gave their own thanks, and sang their own praise. The church was filled with a crescendo of thousands of cries, raised in supplication and praise. As I experienced this symphony of prayer, I felt all things human being gathered together around the body and blood of Christ and made into one great Eucharistic Prayer.

All the people became priests and lifted up their lives together with the bread and the wine. The people became one body, the

body of Christ, dying on the cross and rising again in glory. Misery and delight, despair and hope, fear and love, death and life —
all became one in this wave of prayer that finally flowed into the prayer that Jesus himself taught us, the Our Father. "I want you to come to pray with me and my people," John had said. Now I saw what he meant and recognized better than ever before that we must make our lives into one unceasing prayer.

— *Love in a Fearful Land,* 95–96

From Mind to Heart

How do we concretely go about setting our hearts on God's Kingdom? When I lie in my bed, not able to fall asleep because of my many worries, when I do my work preoccupied about all the things that can go wrong, when I can't get my mind off my concern for a dying friend — what am I supposed to do! Set my heart on the Kingdom? Fine, but how does one do this? . . .

One simple answer is to move from the mind to the heart by slowly saying a prayer with as much attentiveness as possible. This may sound like offering a crutch to someone who asks you to heal his broken leg. The truth, however, is that a prayer, prayed from the heart, heals. When you know the Our Father, the Apostles' Creed, the "Glory Be to the Father" by heart, you have something to start with. You might like to learn by heart the Twenty-third Psalm: "The Lord is my shepherd . . . " or Paul's words about love to the Corinthians or St. Francis's prayer: "Lord, make me an instrument of your peace. . . . " As you lie in your bed, drive your car, wait for the bus, or walk your dog, you can slowly let the words of one of these prayers go through your mind simply trying to listen with your whole being to what they are saying. You will be constantly distracted by your worries, but if you keep going back to the words of the prayer, you will gradually discover that your worries become less obsessive and that you really start to enjoy praying. And as the prayer descends from your mind into the center of your being you will discover its healing power.   — *Here and Now,* 90–93

Prayer: Three Rules

To come to an answer to the personal question: "What is the prayer of my heart?" we first of all have to know how to find this most personal prayer. Where do we look, what do we do, to whom do we go in order to discover how we — as individual human beings with our own history, our own milieu, our own character, our own insights, and our own freedom to act — are called to enter into intimacy with God? The question about the prayer of our heart is, in fact, the question about our own most personal vocation.

...It seems possible to establish a few guidelines. A careful look at the lives of people for whom prayer was indeed "the only thing needed" (see Luke 10:42) shows that three "rules" are always observed: a contemplative reading of the word of God, a silent listening to the voice of God, and a trusting obedience to a spiritual guide. Without the Bible, without silent time, and without someone to direct us, finding our own way to God is very hard and practically impossible....

To take the Holy Scriptures and read them is the first thing we have to do to open ourselves to God's call. Reading the Scriptures is not as easy as it seems since in our academic world we tend to make anything and everything we read subject to analysis and discussion. But the word of God should lead us first of all to contemplation and meditation. Instead of taking the words apart, we should bring them together in our innermost being; instead of wondering if we agree or disagree, we should wonder which words are directly spoken to us and connect directly with our most personal story. Instead of thinking about the words as potential subjects for an interesting dialogue or paper, we should be willing to let them penetrate into the most hidden corners of our heart, even to those places where no other word has yet found entrance....

Secondly, we simply need quiet time in the presence of God. Although we want to make all our time, time for God, we will never succeed if we do not reserve a minute, an hour, a morning, a day, a week, a month, or whatever period of time for God and him alone. This asks for much discipline and risk taking because we always seem to have something more urgent to do and "just sitting there" and "doing nothing" often disturbs us more than it helps. But there is no way around this. Being useless and silent in the presence of our God belongs to the core of all prayer....

Contemplative reading of the Holy Scriptures and silent time in the presence of God belong closely together. The word of God draws us into silence; silence makes us attentive to God's word....

But word and silence both need guidance. How do we know that we are not deluding ourselves, that we are not selecting those words that best suit our passions, that we are not just listening to the voice of our own imagination? Many have quoted the Scriptures and many have heard voices and seen visions in silence, but only a few have found their way to God. Who can be the judge in his own case? Who can determine if his feelings and insights are leading him in the right direction. Our God is greater than our own heart and mind, and too easily we are tempted to make our heart's desires and our mind's speculations into the will of God. Therefore, we need a guide, a director, a counselor who helps us to distinguish between the voice of God and all the other voices coming from our own confusion or from dark powers far beyond our control. We need someone who encourages us when we are tempted to give it all up, to forget it all, to just walk away in despair.... We need someone who can suggest to us when to read and when to be silent, which words to reflect upon and what to do when silence creates much fear and little peace.

— *Reaching Out*, 96–99

SILENCE AND THE WORD

Word Out of Silence

O Lord Jesus, your words to your Father were born out of your silence. Lead me into this silence, so that my words may be spoken in your name and thus be fruitful. It is so hard to be silent, silent with my mouth, but even more, silent with my heart. There is so much talking going on within me. It seems that I am always involved in inner debates with myself, my friends, my enemies, my supporters, my opponents, my colleagues, and my rivals. But this inner debate reveals how far my heart is from you. If I were simply to rest at your feet and realize that I belong to you and you alone, I would easily stop arguing with all the real and imagined people around me. These arguments show my insecurity, my fear, my apprehensions, and my need for being recognized and receiving attention. You, O Lord, will give me all the attention I need if I would simply stop talking and start listening to you. I know that in the silence of my heart you will speak to me and show me your love. Give me, O Lord, that silence. Let me be patient and grow slowly into this silence in which I can be with you. Amen.   — A Cry for Mercy, 18

Power of the Word

Words, my own included, have lost their creative power. Their limitless multiplication has made us lose confidence in words and caused us to think, more often than not, "They are just words."

Teachers speak to students for six, twelve, eighteen, and sometimes twenty-four years. But the students often emerge from the experience with the feeling, "They were just words." Preachers preach their sermons week after week and year after year. But their parishioners remain the same and often think, "They are just words." Politicians, businessmen, ayatollahs, and popes give speeches and make statements "in season and out of season," but those who listen say: "They are just words, just another distraction."

The result of this is that the main function of the word, which is communication, is no longer realized. The word no longer communicates, no longer fosters communion — no longer creates community — and therefore no longer gives life. The word no longer offers trustworthy ground on which people can meet each other and build society.

Do I exaggerate? Let us focus for a moment on theological education. What else is the goal of theological education than to bring us closer to the Lord our God so that we may be more faithful to the great commandment to love him with all our heart, with all our soul, and with all our mind, and our neighbor as ourselves (Matt. 22:37)? Seminaries and divinity schools must lead theology students into an ever-growing communion with God, with each other, and with their fellow human beings. Theological education is meant to form our whole person toward an increasing conformity with the mind of Christ so that our way of praying and our way of believing will be one.

But is this what takes place? Often it seems that we who study or teach theology find ourselves entangled in such a complex network of discussions, debates, and arguments about God and "God-issues" that a simple conversation with God or a simple presence to God has become practically impossible. Our heightened verbal ability, which enables us to make many distinctions, has sometimes become a poor substitute for a single-minded commitment to the Word who is life. If there is a crisis in theological education, it is first and foremost a crisis of the word. This is not to say that critical intellectual work and the subtle distinctions it requires have no place in theological training. But when our words are no longer a reflection of the divine Word in and through whom the world has been created and redeemed, they lose their grounding and become as seductive and misleading as the words used to sell Geritol.

There was a time when the obvious milieu for theological education was the monastery. There words were born out of silence and could lead one deeper into silence. Although monasteries are no longer the most common places of theological education, silence remains as indispensable today as it was in the past. The Word of God is born out of the eternal silence of God, and it is to this Word out of silence that we want to be witnesses.

—*The Way of the Heart*, 32–33

The Silent Pilgrim

Abba Tithoes once said, "Pilgrimage means that a man should control his tongue." The expression "to be on pilgrimage is to be silent" (*peregrinatio est tacere*) expresses the conviction of the desert fathers that silence is the best anticipation of the future world. The most frequent argument for silence is simply that words lead to sin...clearly expressed by the apostle James: "Every one of us does something wrong, over and over again; the only man who could reach perfection would be someone who never said anything wrong — he would be able to control every part of himself" (James 3:2).

James leaves little doubt that speaking without sinning is very difficult and that, if we want to remain untouched by the sins of the world on our journey to our eternal home, silence is the safest way....[And] St. Benedict not only warns his brothers against evil talk, but also tells them to avoid good, holy, edifying words because, as it is written in the book of Proverbs, "A flood of words is never without its faults" (Prov. 10:19). Speaking is dangerous and easily leads us away from the right path....In short, words can give us the feeling of having stopped too long at one of the little villages that we pass on our journey, of having been motivated more by curiosity than by service. Words often make us forget that we are pilgrims called to invite others to join us on the journey. *Peregrinatio est tacere.* "To be silent keeps us pilgrims."
— *The Way of the Heart*, 36–37

Being Silent with Friends

The thought keeps coming to me that it is as important to be silent with friends as it is to speak with them. Seeing so many people and talking with them about all that has happened and is happening to them often leaves me with a sense that we are not really being together. The exchange of countless details about people's lives can often create more distance than closeness. Words are important in bringing hearts together, but too many words can alienate us from one another.

I feel an increasing desire to be silent with friends. Not every event has to be told, not every idea has to be shared. Once an atmosphere of mutual trust is present we can be silent together and let the Lord be the one who speaks, gently and softly.

Listening together to Jesus is a very powerful way to grow closer to each other and to reach a level of intimacy that no interpersonal exchange of words can bring about. A silence lived together in the presence of Jesus will also continue to bear many fruits in the future. It seems that a caring silence can enter deeper into our memory than many caring words.

— *The Primacy of the Heart,* 41

The Transforming Word

We live in a world where words are cheap. Words engulf us. In advertisements, on billboards and traffic signs, in pamphlets, booklets, and books, on blackboards, overhead projectors, flip charts, screens, and newsrunners. Words move, flicker, turn around, grow bigger, brighter, and fatter. They are presented to us in all sizes and colors — but finally we say, "Well, they are just words." Increased in number, words have decreased in value. Their main value seems to be informational. Words inform us. We need words in order to know what to do or how to do it, where to go and how to get there.

It is not surprising, then, that the words in the Eucharist are listened to mostly as words that inform us. They tell us a story, they instruct, they admonish. Since most of us have heard these words before, they seldom touch us deeply. Often we scarcely pay attention to them; they have become too familiar. We don't expect to be surprised or touched. We listen to them as to "the same old story" — whether read from a book or spoken from a pulpit.

The tragedy is that the word then loses its sacramental quality. The Word of God is sacramental. That means it is sacred, and as a sacred word it makes present what it indicates. When Jesus spoke to the two sad travelers on the road and explained to them the words of Scriptures that were about himself, their hearts began to burn, that is to say, they experienced his presence. Speaking about himself he became present to them. With his words he did much more than simply make them think of him, or instruct them about himself, or inspire them with his memory. Through his words he became really present to them. This is what we mean by the sacramental quality of the word. The word creates what it expresses.

The Word of God is always sacramental. In the book of Genesis we are told that God created the world, but in Hebrew the words for "speaking" and for "creating" are the same word. Literally translated it says, "God spoke light and light was." For God, speaking is creating. When we say that God's word is sacred, we mean that God's word is full of God's presence.... Often we think about the word as an exhortation to go out and change our lives. But the full power of the word lies, not in how we apply it to our lives after we have heard it, but in its transforming power that does its divine work as we listen.

The Gospels are filled with examples of God's presence in the word. Personally, I am always touched by the story of Jesus in the synagogue of Nazareth. There he read from Isaiah: "The Spirit of the Lord is on me, for he has anointed me to bring good news to the afflicted. He has sent me to proclaim liberation to captives, sight to the blind, to let the oppressed go free, to proclaim a year of favor from the Lord" (Luke 4:18–13).

After having read these words, Jesus said, "This text is being fulfilled today even while you are listening." Suddenly, it becomes clear that the afflicted, the captives, the blind, and the oppressed are not people somewhere outside of the synagogue who, someday, will be liberated; they are the people who are listening. And it is in the listening that God becomes present and heals.

The Word of God is not a word to apply in our daily lives at some later date; it is a word to heal us through, and in, our listening here and now.   — *With Burning Hearts,* 44–47

SOLITUDE

The Furnace of Transformation

Solitude is the furnace of transformation. Without solitude we remain victims of our society and continue to be entangled in the illusions of the false self. Jesus himself entered into this furnace.

There he was tempted with the three compulsions of the world: to be relevant ("turn stones into loaves"), to be spectacular ("throw yourself down"), and to be powerful ("I will give you all these kingdoms"). There he affirmed God as the only source of his identity. ("You must worship the Lord your God and serve him alone.") Solitude is the place of the great struggle and the great encounter — the struggle against the compulsions of the false self and the encounter with the loving God who offers himself as the substance of the new self.

Solitude is not a private therapeutic place. Rather, it is the place of conversion, the place where the old self dies and the new self is born, the place where the emergence of the new man and the new woman occurs.

In solitude I get rid of my scaffolding: no friends to talk with, no telephone calls to make, no meetings to attend, no music to entertain, no books to distract, just me — naked, vulnerable, weak, sinful, deprived, broken — nothing. It is this nothingness that I have to face in my solitude, a nothingness so dreadful that everything in me wants to run to my friends, my work, and my distractions so that I can forget my nothingness and make myself believe that I am worth something. But that is not all. As soon as I decide to stay in my solitude, confusing ideas, disturbing images, wild fantasies, and weird associations jump about in my mind like monkeys in a banana tree.... The task is to persevere in my solitude, to stay in my cell until all my seductive visitors get tired of pounding on my door and leave me alone.

It is the struggle to die to the false self. But this struggle is far, far beyond our own strength. Anyone who wants to fight his demons with his own weapons is a fool.... Only Christ can overcome the powers of evil. Only in and through him can we survive the trials of our solitude.... As we come to realize that it is not we who live, but Christ who lives in us, that he is our true self, we can slowly let our compulsions melt away and begin to experience the freedom of the children of God....

We have to fashion our own desert where we can withdraw every day, shake off our compulsions, and dwell in the gentle healing presence of our Lord.

Solitude is not simply a means to an end. Solitude is its own end. It is the place where Christ remodels us in his own image and frees us from the victimizing compulsions of the world. Solitude is the place of our salvation.   —*The Way of the Heart,* 13–17

Solitude and Community

Solitude is not private time in contrast to time together, nor a time to restore our tired minds. Solitude is very different from a time-out from community life. Solitude is the ground from which community grows. When we pray alone, study, read, write, or simply spend quiet time away from the places where we interact with each other directly, we enter into a deeper intimacy with each other. It is a fallacy to think that we grow closer to each other only when we talk, play, or work together. Much growth certainly occurs in such human interactions, but these interactions derive their fruit from solitude, because in solitude our intimacy with each other is deepened. In solitude we discover each other in a way that physical presence makes difficult if not impossible. There we recognize a bond with each other that does not depend on words, gestures, or actions, a bond much deeper than our own efforts can create....

Solitude is essential for community life because there we begin to discover a unity that is prior to all unifying actions. In solitude we become aware that we were together before we came together and that community life is not a creation of our will but an obedient response to the reality of our being united. Whenever we enter into solitude, we witness to a love that transcends our interpersonal communications and proclaims that we love each other because we have been loved first (1 John 4:19).... Solitude creates that free community that makes bystanders say, "See how they love each other."   —*Clowning in Rome,* 13–15

A Discipline

Walks in nature, the repetition of short prayers such as the Jesus prayer, simple forms of chanting, certain movements or postures — these and many other elements can become a helpful part of the discipline of solitude. But we have to decide which particular form of this discipline best fits us, to which we can remain faithful. It is better to have a daily practice of ten minutes of solitude than to have a whole hour once in a while. It is better to become familiar with one posture than to keep experimenting with different ones. Simplicity and regularity are the best guides in finding our way. They allow us to make the discipline of solitude as much a part of our daily lives as eating and sleeping. When that happens, our noisy worries will slowly lose their power over us and the renewing activity of God's Spirit will slowly make its presence known.

Although the discipline of solitude asks us to set aside time and space, what finally matters is that our hearts become like quiet cells where God can dwell, wherever we go and whatever we do.
— *Making All Things New*, 78–79

Creativity Out of Loneliness

I wonder if not all creativity asks for a certain encounter with our loneliness. And it is fear of this encounter which severely limits our possible self-expression. When I have to write an article and face a white, empty sheet of paper, I nearly have to tie myself to the chair to keep me from consulting one more book before putting my own words on paper. And after a busy day when I am alone and free, I have to fight the urge not to make one more trip to the mailbox, one more phone call, or one more visit to a friend who will entertain me for the last few hours of the day. And when I think of the day, I sometimes wonder if the educational enterprise, so full with lectures, seminars, conferences, requirements, papers, and examinations, has in fact become one big distraction, once in a while entertaining, but mostly preventing us from facing our lonely self, which is our main source of search and research.

The first task of educational institutions should be to protect the privilege of being school, *escola,* that means, free time for

those who want to understand themselves and their world a little
better.... — "The Lonely Search for God" (audiotape)

A Family Vocation

The first and perhaps most mysterious vocation of the family is to
offer solitude. Solitude is the first gift of man, woman, and children to each other: "Never try to suppress the Spirit," says Paul.
In solitude the Spirit reveals itself to us, and it becomes possible
to "pray constantly and be joyful at all times." In solitude we
discover the inner space where our creativity finds its roots and
from which our real vitality springs....

We live in a world where we are made to believe that we *are*
what we *do*. We are important if we do something important; we
are intelligent if we do something intelligent; we are valuable if
we do something valuable. Therefore, we are very concerned to
have something to do, to be occupied. And if we are not occupied, we are usually preoccupied, that is, busy with a worrying
mind. But when we live as if we *are* what we *do*, we have sold
our soul to the world. We have allowed the world to determine
who we are. We have, in fact, become lonely people, always anxiously looking around and wondering what other people think
about us, always needing people to consider us nice, intelligent,
and worthwhile....

Therefore, the first gift of family members to each other is the
gift of solitude in which they can discover their real selves. A
family built on false selves, selves put together from occupation
and preoccupation, judgments and opinions, is doomed to failure. Only to the degree that the members of a family allow each
other to discover their real selves in solitude can real love exist.
The family is the place where solitude kisses solitude, where, as
Rilke says, "Solitudes salute each other."

— "Spirituality and the Family," 7

2

Embracing Our Lives

This section explores in more detail the inner struggle to let go of our superficial identities and to accept our true identity as children of God. The all-important moment in our spiritual lives is when we understand that we are truly God's beloved. With that moment as a starting point, Henri encourages us to stop running away from ourselves and to receive deeply the message of belovedness into all parts of our lives, especially those parts of ourselves of which we are ashamed. The path to conversion must include a progressive and total befriending of our brokenness. In this self-befriending we move from our more superficial, socially constructed, false selves, to our true selves, given by God. Henri dedicated the last ten years of his life to the L'Arche community of handicapped people. Bill's story (see below, p. 32) illustrates one way in which this community helps its members find their true loveliness in God.

The conversion to our authentic identities opens up a surprising new experience of time which the Gospels call "eternal life." In our true selves, we live no longer bound by a life of mere chronology, but actually share in God's eternity. Thus, our "end" in chronological death is really not an end at all, but a doorway into a wider participation in God and in the lives of those we love.

BEING THE BELOVED

The Commercialization of Love

The most important thing you can say about God's love is that God loves us not because of anything we've done to earn that love, but because God, in total freedom, has decided to love us. At first sight, this doesn't seem to be very inspiring, but if you reflect on it more deeply this thought can affect and influence your life greatly. We're inclined to see our whole existence in terms of *quid pro quo;* you scratch my back, and I'll scratch yours. We begin by assuming that people will be nice to us if we are nice to them; that they will help us if we help them; that they will invite us if we invite them; that they will love us if we love them. And so the conviction is deeply rooted in us that being loved is something you have to earn. In our pragmatic and utilitarian times this conviction has become even stronger. We can scarcely conceive of getting something for nothing. Everything has to be worked for, even a kind word, an expression of gratitude, a sign of affection.

I think it's this mentality that lies behind a lot of anxiety, unrest, and agitation. It's as though we're forever on the go, trying to prove to each other that we deserve to be loved. The doubt we harbor within us drives us on to ever greater activity. In that way we try to keep our heads above water and not drown in our ever increasing lack of self-respect. The enormous propensity to seek recognition, admiration, popularity, and renown is rooted in the fear that, without all this, we are worthless. You could call it the "commercialization" of love. Nothing for nothing. Not even love.

The result is a state of mind that makes us live as though our worth as human beings depended on the way others react to us. We allow other people to determine who we are. We think we're good if other people find us to be so; we think we're intelligent if others consider us intelligent; we think we're religious if others think so too....

Thus, we sell our souls to the world. We're no longer master in our own house. Our friends and enemies decide who we are. We've become the playthings of their good or bad opinions....

The tragic thing, though, is that we humans aren't capable of dispelling one another's loneliness and lack of self-respect. We humans haven't the capacity to relieve one another's most radical predicament. Our ability to satisfy one another's deepest longing is so limited that time and time again we are in danger of disappointing one another....

Everything that Jesus has done, said, and undergone is meant to show us that the love we most long for is given to us by God, not because we've deserved it, but because God is a God of love....

If we had a firm faith in God's unconditional love for us, it would no longer be necessary to be always on the lookout for ways of being admired by people, and we would need, even less, to obtain from people by force what God desires to give us so abundantly....   — *Letters to Marc*, 49–52

Original Goodness

For a very long time I considered low self-esteem to be some kind of virtue. I had been warned so often against pride and conceit that I came to consider it a good thing to deprecate myself.

But now I realize that the real sin is to deny God's first love for me, to ignore my original goodness. Because without claiming that first love and that original goodness for myself, I lose touch with my true self and embark on the destructive search among the wrong people and in the wrong places for what can only be found in the house of my Father.

I do not think I am alone in this struggle to claim God's first love and my original goodness. Beneath much human assertiveness, competitiveness, and rivalry, beneath much self-confidence and even arrogance, there is often a very insecure heart, much less sure of itself than outward behavior would lead one to believe. I have often been shocked to discover that men and women with obvious talents and with many rewards for their accomplishments have so many doubts about their own goodness. Instead of experiencing their outward successes as a sign of their inner beauty, they live them as a cover-up for their sense of personal worthlessness. Not a few have said to me: "If people only knew what goes on in my innermost self, they would stop with their applause and praise."

...Many [people] have horrendous stories that offer very plausible reasons for their low self-esteem: stories about parents who were not giving them what they needed, about teachers who mistreated them, about friends who betrayed them, and about a church which left them out in the cold during a critical moment of their life.

The parable of the prodigal son is a story that speaks about a love that existed before any rejection was possible and that will still be there after all rejections have taken place. It is the first and everlasting love of a God who is Father as well as Mother. It is the fountain of all true human love, even the most limited. Jesus' whole life and preaching had only one aim: to reveal this inexhaustible, unlimited motherly and fatherly love of his God and to show the way to let that love guide every part of our daily lives.   — *The Return of the Prodigal Son*, 101–2

Our True Identity (a sermon)

At the core of my faith belongs the conviction that we are the beloved sons and daughters of God. And one of the enormous spiritual tasks we have is to claim that and to live a life based on that knowledge. And that's not very easy. In fact, most of us fail constantly to claim the truth of who we are.

I might draw a line on a flip chart and say, "That's my life, my little chronology, my little clocktime. Well, I was born in 1932, and I wonder where the end point will be? Maybe 2010, not so bad." But that's really all I have. Now, you may draw your beginning point a little further to the right, and say "I came here." And you may draw your end point a little to the right of mine and say, "I have a few more years here." But it doesn't make very much difference. It's still a small, little life that you have. A little life that goes by very, very fast.

The question for you and me is "Who are we?" Because that's the question that keeps us going. All during our lives we try to answer that question: "Who am I?"

The first answer we often come up with is "I am what I do." And this is very real. When I do good things and have a little success in life, I feel good about myself. But when I fail I start getting low or depressed. And when I get older I can't do much, so I say "Look what I did in my life...look, look, look, I did something good."

Or we might say, "I am what other people say about me." This is very powerful, what people say about you. In fact, it is sometimes most important. When people speak well of you, you can walk around quite freely. But when somebody starts saying negative things about you, you might start feeling sad. I remember speaking to thousands of people, and they would say, "That was wonderful, what you said." But one person stands up and says, "Hey, I thought it was a lot of nonsense." And that is the only person I remember. Sometimes, it is when someone talks against you that it can cut deep into your heart. And when someone in the morning says something about you that is hurtful,...it can stay with you the whole day and ruin your mood.

And you might also say, "I am what I have." For example, I am a Dutch person, with kind parents, with good education and good health. But as soon as I lose any of it,...if a family member dies, or my health goes, or if I lose the property I have, then I can slip into inner darkness....

Quite often, a lot of your and my energy goes into "I am what I do," "I am what others say about me," "I am what I have." And you know, when that's the case, our life quickly becomes a repetitive up and down motion. Because when people speak well about me and when I do good things and when I have a lot, I am quite up and excited. But when I start losing, when suddenly I find out that I can't do anything anymore, when I suddenly find out that people talk against me, when I find that I lose my friends, I might slip into depression and be very low. And before you realize it, you and I are on a zigzag. Up and down. And most of our work, our mental energy is an attempt to stay above the line, and we call that surviving. We want to hold on to our good name, hold on to some good work, hold on to our property, but we know that in the end there is the word that says, "We are going to die after all."

And you know, when you live this kind of life, with all these ups and downs, the end is death. And when you are dead, you're dead. Nobody talks about you anymore, you don't have anything anymore, you can't do anything anymore. You lose it all. And that little life of yours and mine has come to nothing. And what I want to say to you today is that this whole thing is wrong. That that is not who you are, and it is not who I am.

That is what the demon said to Jesus when he went to the desert. He said, "Turn the stones into bread and show that you can do something." "Jump from the temple and let people catch you so they speak well of you." "Kneel in front of me and I will give you a lot of possessions." Then you are loved. Because you do something, people speak well of you, . . . and everybody is going to love you. But Jesus says, "That is a lie. That's the greatest lie that makes you and me enter into relationships of violence and destruction."

Because I know who I am. I know who I am. Because before the Spirit sent me to be tempted, the Spirit came upon me and said, "You are the beloved Child. You are my beloved Son. On you my favor rests." That's who you are. That's who I am. And Jesus heard that voice. "You are my beloved. On you my favor rests."

And it was that voice that he clung to as he lived his life. And people praised him, and people rejected him, and people said Hosanna, and people crucified him. But Jesus held on to the truth. "Whatever happens, I am the beloved of God, and that is who I am." And that allows me to live in a world that keeps rejecting me or praising me or laughing at me or spitting on me. I am the beloved. Not because people say I'm great, but because I am the beloved, even before I was born.

And dear friends, if there is anything that I want you to hear, it is that what is said of Jesus is said of you. You have to hear that you are the beloved daughter or son of God. And to hear it not only in your head but in your gut, to hear it so that your whole life can be turned around.

We go to the Scriptures. "I have loved you with an everlasting love. I have written your name in the palm of my hand from all eternity. I have molded you in the depths of the earth and knitted you in your mother's womb. I love you. I embrace you. You are mine and I am yours and you belong to me." You have to hear this, because if you can hear this voice that speaks to you from all eternity to all eternity, then your life will become more and more the life of the beloved, because that's who you are.

And then you start discovering that all that you do in this chronology is nurtured from the knowledge that you are the beloved. That that is who you are. And when you start believing in this, then this spiritual knowledge will become bigger until it transforms your daily life. You will still have rejections and you will still have praise and losses, but you will live them no longer as a person searching for his or her identity. You will live them as the beloved. You will live your pain and your anguish and your successes and your failures as the one who knows who you are.

And I want to give you a little word here. The voice of the one who calls you the beloved is the voice of the first love. John writes, "Love one another because God has loved you first" (15:12). And the great struggle is to claim that first love. You were loved before your father and your mother and your brother and your sister and your teachers loved you.... The people who love us don't always love us well.... The people who care for us also wound us. And you might know from your experience that the people who are closest to you, like your father, mother, children, brother, teachers, churches, are also the ones who might hurt you most. And how to live that? How to live the naked truth that in this world love and wounds are never separated? We can only live it when we always reclaim that first love.

Therefore, we can forgive those who love us poorly, and we can recognize in the love that we do receive a hint or glimpse of the first love as real. Could you hold on to that? Every time that you have a temptation to become bitter or jealous, to lash out, to feel rejected, can you go back and say, "No, I am the beloved daughter of God." And even though I am rejected, that rejection should become for me a way to reclaim the truth. It should be like a pruning that helps me to claim more fully and deeply the truth of my belovedness. And if I can hold on to that and live in the world, then I can be free to love other people without expecting them to give me all that my heart desires.

Because God has created you and me with a heart that only God's love can satisfy. And every other love will be partial, will be real, but limited, will be painful. And if we are willing to let the pain prune us, to give us a deeper sense of our belovedness, then we can be as free as Jesus and walk on this world and proclaim God's first love, wherever we go.

—Sermon, "Being the Beloved," August 23, 1992,
delivered on Robert Schuller's *Hour of Power*

Voice of Despair, Voice of Love

Judas and Peter present me with the choice between running away from Jesus in despair or returning to him in hope. Judas betrayed Jesus and hanged himself. Peter denied Jesus and returned to him in tears.

Sometimes despair seems an attractive choice, solving everything in the negative. The voice of despair says, "I sin over and over again. After endless promises to myself and others to do better next time, I find myself back again in the old dark places. Forget about trying to change. I have tried for years. It didn't work and it will never work. It is better that I get out of people's way, be forgotten, no longer around, dead."

This strangely attractive voice takes all uncertainties away and puts an end to the struggle. It speaks unambiguously for the darkness and offers a clear-cut negative identity.

But Jesus came to open my ears to another voice that says, "I am your God, I have molded you with my own hands, and I love what I have made. I love you with a love that has no limits, because I love you as I am loved. Do not run away from me. Come back to me — not once, not twice, but always again. You are my child. How can you ever doubt that I will embrace you again, hold you against my breast, kiss you and let my hands run through your hair? I am your God — the God of mercy and compassion, the God of pardon and love, the God of tenderness and care. Please do not say that I have given up on you, that I cannot stand you anymore, that there is no way back. It is not true. I so much want you to be with me. I so much want you to be close to me. I know all your thoughts. I hear all your words. I see all of your actions. And I love you because you are beautiful, made in my own image, an expression of my most intimate love.

Do not judge yourself. Do not condemn yourself. Do not reject yourself. Let my love touch the deepest, most hidden corners of your heart and reveal to you your own beauty, a beauty that you have lost sight of, but which will become visible to you again in the light of my mercy. Come, come, let me wipe your tears, and let my mouth come close to your ear and say to you, "I love you, I love you, I love you."

This is the voice that Jesus wants us to hear. It is the voice that calls us always to return to the one who has created us in love and wants to re-create us in mercy.

— *The Road to Daybreak*, 157–58

A Discipline of Becoming

If it is true that we not only *are* the beloved, but also have *to become* the beloved; if it is true that we not only are children of God, but also have to become children of God; if it is true that we not only are brothers and sisters, but also have to become brothers and sisters — if all that is true, how then can we get a grip on this process of becoming? If the spiritual life is not simply a way of being, but also a way of becoming, what then is the nature of this becoming?

...Becoming the beloved means letting the truth of our belovedness become en-fleshed in everything we think, say, or do. It entails a long and painful process of appropriation or, better, incarnation. As long as "being the beloved" is little more than a beautiful thought or a lofty idea that hangs above my life to keep me from becoming depressed, nothing really changes. What is required is *to become* the beloved in the commonplaces of my daily existence and, bit by bit, to close the gap that exists between what I know myself to be and the countless specific realities of everyday life. Becoming the beloved is pulling the truth revealed to me from above down into the ordinariness of what I am, in fact, thinking of, talking about, and doing from hour to hour.

— Life of the Beloved, 38

DRINKING OUR CUP

Choosing Our Lives

Drinking the cup of life makes our own everything we are living. It is saying, "This is my life," but also "I want this to be my life." Drinking the cup of life is fully appropriating and internalizing our own unique existence, with all its sorrows and joys.

It is not easy to do this. For a long time we might not feel capable of accepting our own life; we might keep fighting for a better or at least a different life. Often a deep protest against our "fate" rises in us. We didn't choose our country, our parents, the color of our skin, our sexual orientation. We didn't even choose our character, intelligence, physical appearance, or mannerisms. Sometimes we want to do every possible thing to change the circumstances of our life. We wish we were in another body, lived in another time, or had another mind! A cry can come out of our depths: "Why do I have to be this person? I didn't ask for it, and I don't want it."

But as we gradually come to befriend our own reality, to look with compassion at our own sorrows and joys, and as we are able to discover the unique potential of our way of being in the world, we can move beyond our protest, put the cup of our life to our lips and drink it, slowly, carefully, but fully.

Often when we wish to comfort people, we say: "Well, it is sad this has happened to you, but try to make the best of it."

But "making the best of it" is not what drinking the cup is about. Drinking our cup is not simply adapting ourselves to a bad situation and trying to use it as well as we can. Drinking our cup is a hopeful, courageous, and self-confident way of living. It is standing in the world with head erect, solidly rooted in the knowledge of who we are, facing the reality that surrounds us, and responding to it from our hearts.

— *Can You Drink the Cup?* 81–82

Complaining Is Self-Rejection

When I listen carefully to the words with which the elder son attacks his father — self-righteous, self-pitying, jealous words — I hear a deeper complaint. It is the complaint that comes from a heart that feels it never received what it was due. It is the complaint expressed in countless subtle and not-so-subtle ways, forming a bedrock of human resentment. It is the complaint that cries out: "I tried so hard, worked so long, did so much, and still I have not received what others get so easily. Why do people not thank me, not invite me, not play with me, not honor me, while they pay so much attention to those who take life so easily and so casually?"

It is in this spoken or unspoken complaint that I recognize the elder son in me. Often I catch myself complaining about little rejections, little impolitenesses, little negligences. Time and again I discover within me that murmuring, whining, grumbling, lamenting, and griping that go on and on even against my will. The more I dwell on the matters in question, the worse my state becomes....

Of one thing I am sure. Complaining is self-perpetuating and counterproductive. Whenever I express my complaints in the hope of evoking pity and receiving the satisfaction I so much desire, the result is always the opposite of what I tried to get. A complainer is hard to live with, and very few people know how to respond to the complaints made by a self-rejecting person. The tragedy is that, often, the complaint, once expressed, leads to that which is most feared: further rejection.

From this perspective, the elder son's inability to share in the joy of his father becomes quite understandable. When he came home from the fields, he heard music and dancing. He knew there was joy in the household. Immediately, he became suspicious. Once the self-rejecting complaint has formed in us, we lose our spontaneity to the extent that even joy can no longer evoke joy in us. . . . Joy and resentment cannot coexist. The music and dancing, instead of inviting to joy, become a cause for even greater withdrawal.   — *The Return of the Prodigal Son*, 67–68

Bill's Story

One very moving celebration I remember was that of Bill's *Life Story Book*. A *Life Story Book* is a collection of photographs, stories, and letters put together as a sort of biography. When Bill came to Daybreak as a sixteen-year-old, he brought few memories with him. He had had a very troublesome childhood and hardly any consistent experiences of love and friendship. His past was so broken, so painful, and so lonely that he had chosen to forget it. He was a man without a history.

But during twenty-five years at Daybreak, he gradually has become a different person. He has made friends. He has developed a close relationship with a family he can visit on weekends or holidays, joined a bowling club, learned woodworking, and traveled with me to places far and wide. Over the years he has created a life worth remembering. He even found the freedom and the courage to recall some of his painful childhood experiences and to reclaim his deceased parents as people who had given him life and love notwithstanding their limitations.

There was enough material for a *Life Story Book* because now there was a beautiful although painful story to tell. Many friends wrote letters to Bill telling him what they remembered about him. Others sent photographs or newspaper clippings about events he had been part of, and others just made drawings that expressed their love for him. After six months of work, the book was finally ready, and it was time to celebrate, not just the new book but Bill's life, which it symbolized.

Many came together for the occasion in the Dayspring Chapel. Bill held the book and lifted it up for all to see. It was a beautifully colored ring binder with many artistically decorated pages. Although it was Bill's book, it was the work of many people.

Then we blessed the book and Bill, who held it. I prayed that this book might help Bill let many people know what a beautiful man he is and what a good life he was living. I also prayed that Bill would remember all the moments of his life — his joys as well as his sorrows — with a grateful heart.

While I prayed tears started to flow from Bill's eyes. When I finished he threw his arms around me and cried loudly. His tears fell on my shoulder while everyone in the circle looked at us with a deep understanding of what was happening. Bill's life had been lifted up for all to see, and he had been able to say it was a life to be grateful for.

Now Bill takes his *Life Story Book* with him on his trips. He shows it to people as a man who believes his life is not something to be ashamed of. To the contrary, it is a gift for others.

— *Can You Drink the Cup?* 72–74

CONVERSION

The Heart of All Action

As soon as I say, "God exists," my existence no longer can remain in the center, because the essence of the knowledge of God reveals my own existence as deriving its total being from his. That is the true conversion experience. I no longer let the knowledge of my existence be the center from which I derive, project, deduct, or intuit the existence of God; I suddenly or slowly find my own existence revealed to me in and through the knowledge of God. Then it becomes real for me that I can love myself and my neighbor only because God has loved me first. The life-converting experience is not the discovery that I have choices to make that determine the way I live out my existence, but the awareness that my existence itself is not in the center. Once I "know" God, that is, once I experience his love as the love in which all my human experiences are anchored, I can only desire one thing: to be in that love. "Being" anywhere else, then, is shown to be illusory and eventually lethal. . . .

Is it better to be in Bolivia, in Peru, in the United States, or in Holland? Is it better to give a glass of water to a thirsty child or to work on a new world order in which children will no longer beg for water? Is it better to read a book or to walk on the street, to write a letter or bind the wounds of a dying man? Is it better to do this or that, say this or that, think about this or that? All these questions suddenly appear to me as false preoccupations, as a captivity in the illusory concern about my own existence, as an expression of my sick supposition that God depends on me, that his existence is derived from mine.

Nothing is real without deriving its reality from God. This was the great discovery of St. Francis when he suddenly saw the whole world in God's hands and wondered why God didn't drop it. St. Augustine, St. Teresa of Avila, St. John Vianney, and all the saints are saints precisely because for them the order of being was turned around and they saw, felt, and — above all — knew with their heart that outside God nothing is, nothing breathes, nothing moves, and nothing lives.

This makes me aware that the basis of all ministry rests not in the moral life but in the mystical life. The issue is not to live as well as we can, but to let our life be one that finds its source in the divine life.

Instead of saying: "Nothing matters any more, since I know that God exists," the converted person says: "All is now clothed in divine light and therefore nothing can be unimportant." The converted person sees, hears, and understands with a divine eye, a divine ear, a divine heart. The converted person knows himself or herself and all the world in God. The converted person *is* where God is, and from that place everything matters: giving water, clothing the naked, working for a new world order, saying a prayer, smiling at a child, reading a book, and sleeping in peace. All has become different while all remains the same.

—*¡Gracias!* 48–50

Vain Glory to Right Glory

Human glory is the result of being considered better, faster, more beautiful, more powerful, or more successful than others. Glory conferred by people is glory which results from being favorably compared to other people. The better our scores on the scoreboard of life, the more glory we receive. This glory comes with upward mobility. The higher we climb on the ladder of success, the more glory we collect. But this same glory also creates our darkness. Human glory, based on competition, leads to rivalry; rivalry carries within it the beginning of violence; and violence is the way to death. Thus human glory proves to be vain glory, false glory, mortal glory.

How then do we come to see and receive God's glory? In his Gospel, John shows that God chose to reveal his glory to us in his humiliation. That is the good, but also disturbing, news. God, in his infinite wisdom, chose to reveal his divinity to us not through competition, but through compassion, that is, through suffering with us. God chose the way of downward mobility.

Every time Jesus speaks about being glorified and giving glory, he always refers to his humiliation and death. It is through the way of the cross that Jesus gives glory to God, receives glory from God, and makes God's glory known to us. The glory of the resurrection can never be separated from the glory of the cross. The risen Lord always shows us his wounds....

If we truly want to see the glory of God, we must move downward with Jesus. This is the deepest reason for living in solidarity with poor, oppressed, and handicapped people. They are the ones through whom God's glory can manifest itself to us. They show us the way to God, the way to salvation.

— *The Road to Daybreak*, 97–98

Wishing to Hoping

We live in a world where people don't know much about hope. We know about wishes. The whole Christmas period is full of wishes. I wish this, or I want that. It's very concrete: I want a toy or a car or a new job. These are all very specific requests. But hope is precisely to say, "I don't know how God is going to fulfill his promises, but I know that he will, and therefore I can live in the present with the knowledge that he is with me." I can then know and trust that the deepest desires of my being will be fulfilled. This way keeps the future very open.…

Hope has nothing to do with optimism. Many people think that hope is optimism, looking at the positive side of life. But Jesus doesn't speak like that at all. When Jesus talks about the future or the end of the world, he describes wars, people in anguish, nation rising against nation, and earthquakes. There's no place where Jesus says, "One day it will all be wonderful." He talks about enormous agony, but he says, "You, you [my beloved ones] pray unceasingly that you will keep your heart focused on me. Stand with your head erect in the presence of the Son of Man. Don't get distracted by it all. Remain focused." Don't think that things will clean up, and finally there won't be any more pain. Jesus is saying that the world is dark, and will remain dark.

If you live with hope, you can live very much in the present because you can nurture the footprints of God in your heart and life. You already have a sense of what is to come. And the whole of the spiritual life is saying that God is right with us, right now, so that we can wait for his coming, and this waiting is a waiting in hope. But because we wait with hope we know that what we are waiting for is already here. We have to nurture that. Here and now matters because God is a God of the present. And God is God of the present because he is God of Eternity.

Hope is to open yourself up to let God do his work in you in ways that transcend your own imagination. As Jesus said, "When you were young you put your belt on and went where you wanted to go. But when you grow spiritually old, then you stretch out your hands and let others and God lead you where you rather wouldn't go." That's hope, to let yourself be led to new places.   — "A Tribute to Henri Nouwen: 1932–1996,"
an interview by Rev. Brian Stiller

Sadness to Joy

For Jesus, joy is clearly a deeper and more truthful state of life than sorrow. He promises joy as the sign of new life: "You will be sorrowful, but your sorrow will turn to joy. A woman in childbirth suffers, because her time has come; but when she has given birth to the child, she forgets the suffering in her joy that a human being has been born into the world. So it is with you: you are sad now, but I shall see you again, and your hearts will be full of joy, and that joy no one shall take from you" (John 16:20b–22).

Jesus connects joy with the promise of seeing him again. In this sense, it is similar to the joy we experience when a dear friend returns after a long absence. But Jesus makes it clear that joy is more than that. It is "his own joy," flowing from the love he shares with his heavenly Father and leading to completion. "Remain in my love ... so that my own joy may be in you and your joy may be complete" (John 15:9b, 11).

The word "ecstasy" helps us to understand more fully the joy that Jesus offers. The literal meaning of the word can help to guide our thinking about joy. "Ecstasy" comes from the Greek *ekstasis,* which in turn is derived from *ek,* meaning out, and *stasis,* a state of standstill. To be ecstatic literally means to be outside of a static place. Thus, those who live ecstatic lives are always moving away from rigidly fixed situations and exploring new, unmapped dimensions of reality. Here we see the essence of joy. Joy is always new. Whereas there can be old pain, old grief, and old sorrow, there can be no old joy. Old joy is not joy! Joy is always connected with movement, renewal, rebirth, change — in short, with life. *— Lifesigns,* 86–88

Cynicism to Joy

For me, it is amazing to experience daily the radical difference between cynicism and joy. Cynics seek darkness wherever they go. They point always to approaching dangers, impure motives, and hidden schemes. They call trust naive, care romantic, and forgiveness sentimental. They sneer at enthusiasm, ridicule spiritual

fervor, and despise charismatic behavior. They consider themselves realists who see reality for what it truly is and who are
not deceived by "escapist emotions." But in belittling God's joy,
their darkness only calls forth more darkness.

People who have come to know the joy of God do not deny
the darkness, but they choose not to live in it. They claim that
the light that shines in the darkness can be trusted more than the
darkness itself and that a little bit of light can dispel a lot of darkness. They point each other to flashes of light here and there and
remind each other that they reveal the hidden but real presence of
God. They discover that there are people who heal each other's
wounds, forgive each other's offenses, share their possessions,
foster the spirit of community, celebrate the gifts they have received, and live in constant anticipation of the full manifestation
of God's glory.

Every moment of each day I have the chance to choose between cynicism and joy. Every thought I have can be cynical or
joyful. Every word I speak can be cynical or joyful. Every action
can be cynical or joyful. Increasingly, I am aware of all these possible choices, and increasingly I discover that every choice for joy
in turn reveals more joy and offers more reason to make life a
true celebration in the house of the Father.

— *The Return of the Prodigal Son*, 109

Salvation Is Now

"Salvation" is about being saved. But from what do we need
to be saved? The traditional answer — and the good one —
is sin and death. We are entrapped by sin and death as in a
hunter's snare.

When we think for a moment of various addictions — al-
cohol, drug, food, gambling, sex — we get some idea of that
entrapment.... [And] all of us have our obsessions. An idea, a
plan, a hobby can obsess us to such a degree that we become
its slave.... These addictions, compulsions, and obsessions reveal
our entrapments. They show our sinfulness because they take
away our freedom as children of God and thus enslave us in a

cramped, shrunken world. Sin makes us want to create our own lives according to our desires and wishes, ignoring the cup that is given to us. Sin makes us self-indulgent....

[But] salvation is not only a goal for the afterlife. Salvation is a reality of every day that we can taste here and now. When I sit down with Adam and help him eat, chat with Bill about our next trip, have coffee with Susanne and breakfast with David, when I embrace Michael, kiss Patsy, or pray with Gordie, salvation is right there. And when we sit together around the low altar table and I offer to all present the glass cup filled with wine, I can announce with great certainty: "This is the cup of salvation."

— *Can You Drink the Cup?* 89–91

BEFRIENDING OUR BROKENNESS

Live Your Wounds Through

You have been wounded in many ways. The more you open yourself to being healed, the more you will discover how deep your wounds are. You will be tempted to become discouraged, because under every wound you uncover you will find others. Your search for true healing will be a suffering search. Many tears still need to be shed.

But do not be afraid. The simple fact that you are more aware of your wounds shows that you have sufficient strength to face them.

The great challenge is *living* your wounds through instead of *thinking* them through. It is better to cry than to worry, better to feel your wounds deeply than to understand them, better to let them enter into your silence than to talk about them. The choice you face constantly is whether you are taking your hurts to your head or to your heart. In your head you can analyze them, find their causes and consequences, and coin words to speak and write about them. But no final healing is likely to come from that source. You need to let your wounds go down into your heart.

Then you can live them through and discover that they will not destroy you. Your heart is greater than your wounds. . . .

Think of each wound as you would of a child who has been hurt by a friend. As long as that child is ranting and raving, trying to get back at the friend, one wound leads to another. But when the child can experience the consoling embrace of a parent, she or he can live through the pain, return to the friend, forgive, and build up a new relationship. Be gentle with yourself and let your heart be your loving parent as you live your wounds through.

— The Inner Voice of Love, 109–10

Grief, a Birthplace of God's Compassion

It might sound strange to consider grief a way to compassion. But it is. Grief asks me to allow the sins of the world — my own in-cluded — to pierce my heart and make me shed tears, many tears, for them. There is no compassion without many tears. If they can't be tears that stream from my eyes, they have to be at least tears that well up from my heart. When I consider the immense waywardness of God's children, our lust, our greed, our violence, our anger, our resentment, and when I look at them through the eyes of God's heart, I cannot but weep and cry out in grief: "Look, my soul, at the way one human being tries to inflict as much pain on another as possible; look at these people plotting to bring harm to their fellows; look at these parents molesting their children; look at this landowner exploiting his workers; look at the violated women, the misused men, the abandoned children. Look, my soul, at the world; see the concentration camps, the prisons, the nursing homes, the hospitals, and hear the cries of the poor."

This grieving is praying. There are so few mourners left in this world. But grief is the discipline of the heart that sees the sin of the world and knows itself to be the sorrowful price of free-dom without which love cannot bloom. I am beginning to see that much of praying is grieving. This grief is so deep not just because the human sin is so great, but also — and more so — because the divine love is so boundless. To become like the Fa-

ther whose only authority is compassion, I have to shed countless tears and so prepare my heart to receive anyone, whatever their journey has been, and forgive them from that heart.
—The Return of the Prodigal Son, 120–21

Permit Your Pain to Become the Pain

Your pain, deep as it is, is connected with specific circumstances. You do not suffer in the abstract. You suffer because someone hurts you at a specific time and in a specific place. Your feelings of rejection, abandonment, and uselessness are rooted in the most concrete events. In this way all suffering is unique. This is eminently true of the suffering of Jesus. His disciples left him, Pilate condemned him, Roman soldiers tortured and crucified him.

Still, as long as you keep pointing to the specifics, you will miss the full meaning of your pain. You will deceive yourself into believing that if the people, circumstances, and events had been different, your pain would not exist. This might be partly true, but the deeper truth is that the situation which brought about your pain was simply the form in which you came in touch with the human condition of suffering. Your pain is the concrete way in which you participate in the pain of humanity.

Paradoxically, therefore, healing means moving from your pain to *the* pain. When you keep focusing on the specific circumstances of your pain, you easily become angry, resentful, and even vindictive. You are inclined to do something about the externals of your pain in order to relieve it; this explains why you often seek revenge. But real healing comes from realizing that your own particular pain is a share in humanity's pain. That realization allows you to forgive your enemies and enter into a truly compassionate life. That is the way of Jesus, who prayed on the cross: "Father forgive them; they do not know what they are doing" (Luke 23:34). Jesus' suffering, concrete as it was, was the suffering of all humanity. His pain was *the* pain.

Every time you can shift your attention away from the external situation that caused your pain and focus on the pain of humanity in which you participate, your suffering becomes easier

to bear. It becomes a "light burden" and an "easy yoke" (Matt.
11:30). Once you discover that you are called to live in solidarity with the hungry, the homeless, the prisoners, the refugees, the
sick, and the dying, your very personal pain begins to be converted into *the* pain and you find new strength to live it. Herein
lies the hope of all Christians.

— The Inner Voice of Love, 103–4

Our Losses, Everyone's Losses

If there is any word that summarizes well our pain, it is the word
"loss." We have lost so much! Sometimes it even seems that life
is just one long series of losses. When we were born we lost the
safety of the womb, when we went to school we lost the security
of our family life, when we got our first job we lost the freedom of youth, when we got married or ordained we lost the joy
of many options, and when we grew old we lost our good looks,
our old friends, or our fame. When we became weak or ill we lost
our physical independence, and when we die we will lose it all!
And these losses are part of the ordinary life! But whose life is ordinary? The losses that settle themselves deeply in our hearts and
minds are the loss of intimacy through separations, the loss of
safety through violence, the loss of innocence through abuse, the
loss of friends through betrayal, the loss of love through abandonment, the loss of home through war, the loss of well-being
through hunger, heat, and cold, the loss of children through illness or accidents, the loss of country through political upheaval,
and the loss of life through earthquakes, floods, plane crashes,
bombings, and diseases.

What to do with our losses? ... Are we going to convince ourselves or others that our losses are little compared to our gains?
Are we going to blame someone? We do all of these things most
of the time, but there is another possibility: the possibility of
mourning. Yes, we must mourn our losses....

And as we feel the pain of our own losses, our grieving hearts
open our inner eye to a world in which losses are suffered far
beyond our own little world of family, friends, and colleagues. It

is the world of prisoners, refugees, AIDS patients, starving children, and the countless human beings living in constant fear. Then the pain of our crying hearts connects us with the moaning and groaning of a suffering humanity. Then our mourning becomes larger than ourselves.

But in the midst of all this pain, there is a strange, shocking, yet very surprising voice. It is the voice of the one who says: "Blessed are those who mourn: they shall be comforted." That's the unexpected news: there is a blessing hidden in our grief. Not those who comfort are blessed, but those who mourn! Somehow, in the midst of our tears, a gift is hidden. Somehow, in the midst of our mourning, the first steps of the dance take place. Somehow, the cries that well up from our losses belong to our songs of gratitude.   — *With Burning Hearts,* 24–28

The Gifts of the Handicapped

Many who have worked for years with handicapped people will gladly say that they have received more than they have given. Sometimes they will even confess that they have found their true selves by working with the handicapped. Jean Vanier told me a story that symbolizes this beautifully. A few years ago, members of L'Arche made a pilgrimage to the Holy Land. When they arrived at the heavily guarded airport in Israel, Jean-Claude, one of the handicapped men, walked right up to the armed Israeli soldiers and started to give each one a handshake, telling them how glad he was to have arrived in the Holy Land! Indeed, very broken people often allow us to see our true selves hidden behind our uniforms and rifles. They tell us that we are really brothers and sisters, and that arms and weapons do not tell the truth of who we are.

Handicapped people are very vulnerable. They cannot hide their weaknesses and are therefore easy victims of maltreatment and ridicule. But this same vulnerability also allows them to bear ample fruit in the lives of those who receive them. They are grateful people. They know they are dependent on others and show this dependence every moment; but their smiles, embraces, and kisses are offered as spontaneous expressions of thanks. They know that all is pure gift to be thankful for. They are people who need care. When they are locked up in custodial institutions and treated as nobodies, they withdraw and cannot bear fruit. They become overwhelmed by fears and close themselves to others. But when they are given a safe space, with truly caring people whom they can trust, they soon become generous givers who are willing to offer their whole hearts.

Handicapped people help us see the great mystery of fecundity. They pull us out of our competitive, production-oriented lives and remind us that we too are handicapped persons in need of love and care. They tell us in many ways that we too do not need to be afraid of our handicap, that we too can bear fruit as Jesus did when he offered his broken body to his Father.

— Lifesigns, 73–74

Powerlessness

This afternoon at three o'clock, my sister called from Holland to tell me that my sister-in-law had given birth to a daughter who was diagnosed as suffering from Down syndrome. A week ago I wrote about having seen a Down syndrome child in the house of Pete Ruggere's neighbors; yesterday I read about that child in the *Wall Street Journal;* today I have a niece who suffers from the same disease. I called Holland and talked to Heiltjen, my sister-in-law. The baby, she told me, had been born five hours previously, and the doctors had told her immediately about the child's handicap. "With Laura, our lives will be very different from now on," she said. My brother Laurent was not in the hospital when I called, but my sister as well as Heiltjen told me how distressed he was. I still find it hard to appropriate this news. I cannot think about much else than this little child who will become the center of my brother and my sister-in-law's lives and will bring them into a world of which they have never dreamed. It will be a world of constant care and attention; a world of very small progressions; a world of new feelings, emotions, and thoughts; a world of affections that come from places invisible in "normal" people.

I know that Laurent and Heiltjen's love is being tested, not only their love for their new child but even more their love for each other and for their two-year-old daughter, Sarah. I pray tonight for them that they will be able to grow in love because of Laura, and that they will discover in her the presence of God in their lives.

Laura is going to be important for all of us in the family. We have never had a "weak" person among us. We all are hardworking, ambitious, and successful people who seldom have had to experience powerlessness. Now Laura enters and tells us a totally new story, a story of weakness, brokenness, vulnerability, and total dependency. Laura, who always will be a child, will teach us the way of Christ as no one will ever be able to do. I hope and pray that I can be of some support to Laurent and Heiltjen in their long journey with Laura, and that Laura will bring all of us closer together and closer to God.   — *¡Gracias!* 14–15

Living in God's Time

Each time we claim for ourselves the truth of our belovedness, our lives are widened and deepened. As the beloved our lives stretch out *far* beyond the boundaries of our birth and death. We do not simply become the beloved at our birth and cease being the beloved at our death. Our belovedness is eternal. God says to us: "I love you with an everlasting love." This love was there before our fathers and mothers loved us, and it will be there long after our friends have cared for us. It is a divine love, an everlasting love, an eternal love.

Precisely because our true identity is rooted in this unconditional, unlimited, everlasting love, we can escape being victimized by our "clock-time." Clock-time is the time we have in this world. That time can be measured in seconds, minutes, hours, days, weeks, months, and years. Our clock-time, *chronos* in Greek, can become an obsession, especially when all that we are is connected with the clock that keeps ticking whether we are awake or asleep.

I have always been very conscious of my clock-time. Often I

asked myself: "Can I still double my years?" When I was thirty I said: "I can easily live another thirty!" When I was forty, I mused, "Maybe I am only halfway!" Today I can no longer say that, and my question has become: "How am I going to use the few years left to me?" All these concerns about our clock-time come from below. They are based on the presupposition that our chronology is all we have to live. But looked upon from above, from God's perspective, our clock-time is embedded in the timeless embrace of God. Looked upon from above, our years on earth are not simply *chronos* but *kairos* — another Greek word for time — which is the opportunity to claim for ourselves the love that God offers us from eternity to eternity.   — *Here and Now,* 137–39

The Fullness of Time

Jesus came in the fullness of time. He will come again in the fullness of time. Wherever Jesus, the Christ is, time is brought to its fullness.

We often experience our time as empty. We hope that tomorrow, next week, next month, or next year the real things will happen. But sometimes we experience the fullness of time. That is when it seems that time stands still; that past, present, and future become one; that everything is present where we are; and that God, we, and all that is have come together in total unity This is the experience of God's time. "When the completion of the time came [that is, in the fullness of time], God sent his Son, born of a woman" (Gal. 4:4), and in the fullness of time God will "bring everything together under Christ, as head, everything in the heavens and everything on earth" (Eph. 1:10). It is in the fullness of time that we meet God.   — *Bread for the Journey,* December 18

Transparent Time

The contemplative life requires the ongoing movement from opaqueness to transparency in our relationship with time. Time constantly threatens to become our great enemy. In our contemporary society it often seems that not money but time enslaves us.

We say, "I wish I could do all the things that I need to do, but I simply have no time. Just thinking about all the things I have to do today — writing five letters, visiting a friend, practicing my music, making a phone call, going to class, finishing a paper, doing my meditation — just thinking about these makes me tired."

Indeed, it seems that many people feel they no longer have time, but that time has them. They experience themselves as victims of an ongoing pressure to meet deadlines, to be ready on time, or to make it on time. . . .

The contemplative life is a life in which time slowly loses its opaqueness and becomes transparent. This is often a very difficult and slow process, but it is full of re-creating power. To start seeing that the many events of our day, week, or year are not in the way of our search for a full life, but rather the way to it, is a real experience of conversion. If we start discovering that writing letters, attending classes, visiting people, and cooking food are not a series of random events that prevent us from realizing our deepest self, but contain within themselves the transforming power we are looking for, then we are beginning to move from time lived as *chronos* to time lived as *kairos*. *Kairos* means *the opportunity*. It is the right time, the real moment, the chance of our life. When our time becomes *kairos*, it opens up endless new possibilities and offers us a constant opportunity for a change of heart.

In Jesus' life every event becomes *kairos*. He opens his public ministry with the words, "The time has come" (Mark 1:15), and he lives every moment of it as an opportunity. Finally, he announces that his time is near (Mark 26:10) and enters into his last hour as *the kairos*. In so doing he liberates history from its fatalistic chronology. . . .

The contemplative life . . . is not a life that offers a few good moments between the many bad ones, but a life that transforms all our time into a window through which the invisible world becomes visible.

It belongs to the core of all ministry to make time transparent so that in the most concrete circumstances of life we can see that our hour is God's hour and that all time is therefore *kairos*.

— *Clowning in Rome*, 96–97

EMBRACING THE PARADOX

Healing Contradictions

The many contradictions in our lives — such as being home while feeling homeless, being busy while feeling bored, being popular while feeling lonely, being believers while feeling many doubts — can frustrate, irritate, and even discourage us. They make us feel that we are never fully present Every door that opens for us makes us see how many more doors are closed.

But there is another response. These same contradictions can bring us into touch with a deeper longing for the fulfillment of a desire that lives beneath all desires and that only God can satisfy. Contradictions, thus understood, create the friction that can help us move toward God.   — *Bread for the Journey*, April 20

Interruptions and Opportunities

What if our interruptions are in fact our opportunities, if they are challenges to an inner response by which growth takes place and through which we come to the fullness of being?

What if the events of our history are molding us as a sculptor molds his clay, and if it is only in a careful obedience to these molding hands that we can discover our real vocation and become mature people? What if all the unexpected interruptions are in fact the invitations to give up old-fashioned and outmoded styles of living and are opening up new unexplored areas of experience? And finally: what if our history does not prove to be a blind impersonal sequence of events over which we have no control, but rather reveals to us a guiding hand pointing to a personal encounter in which all our hopes and aspirations will reach their fulfillment?

Then our life would indeed be a different life because then fate becomes opportunity, wounds a warning, and paralysis an invitation to search for deeper sources of vitality. Then we can look for hope in the middle of crying cities, burning hospitals, and desperate parents and children. Then we can cast off the temptation of despair and speak about the fertile tree while witnessing the dying of the seed. Then indeed we can break out of the prison of an anonymous series of events and listen to the God of history who speaks to us in the center of our solitude and respond to his ever new call for conversion. — *Reaching Out*, 37

Affirming and Emptying Self

Self-affirmation and self-emptying are not opposites because no man can give away what he does not have. No one can give himself in love when he is not aware of himself. Nobody can come to intimacy without having found his identity. Jesus lived thirty years in a simple family. There he became a man who knew who he was and where he wanted to go. Only then was he ready to empty himself and give his life for others. That is the way of all ministry. Through long and often painful formation and training, the minister has to find his place in life, to discover his own contribution, and to affirm his own self: not to cling to it and claim it as his own unique property, but to go out, offer his services to others, and empty himself so that God can speak through him and call man to new life.

So the identity of the pastor, as it becomes visible in his pastoral care, is born from the intangible tension between self-affirmation and self-denial, self-fulfillment and self-emptying, self-realization and self-sacrifice. There are periods in life in which the emphasis is more on one than on the other, but in general it seems that as a man becomes more mature he will become less concerned with girding himself and more willing to stretch out his hands and to follow him who found his life by losing it.

— *Creative Ministry*, 51

Grateful in the Paradox

Gratitude in its deepest sense means to live life as a gift to be received gratefully. But gratitude as the Gospel speaks about it embraces *all* of life: the good and the bad, the joyful and the painful, the holy and the not so holy. Is this possible in a society where gladness and sadness, joy and sorrow, peace and conflict, remain radically separated? Can we counter the many advertisements that tell us, "You cannot be glad when you are sad, so be happy: buy this, do that, go here, go there, and you will have a moment of happiness during which you can forget your sorrow"? Is it truly possible to embrace with gratitude all of our life and not just the good things that we like to remember?

Jesus calls us to recognize that gladness and sadness are never separate, that joy and sorrow really belong together, and that mourning and dancing are part of the same movement. That is why Jesus calls us to be grateful for every moment that we have lived and to claim our unique journey as God's way to mold our hearts to greater conformity with God's own. The cross is the main symbol of our faith, and it invites us to find hope where we see pain and to reaffirm the resurrection where we see death. The call to be grateful is a call to trust that every moment of our life can be claimed as the way of the cross that leads us to new life. When the disciples were on the way to Emmaus and met Jesus, they could not believe that there was much fruit to be expected from all the suffering they had witnessed. But Jesus revealed that it was precisely because of the suffering and pain that new life was born. It is so easy for me to put the bad memories under the rug of my life and to think only about the good things that please me. By doing so, however, I prevent myself from discovering the joy beneath my sorrow, the peace hidden in the midst of my conflicts, and the strength that becomes visible in the midst of my weakness.   — "All Is Grace," 39–40

Celebrating the Paradox

When we speak about celebration we tend rather easily to bring to mind happy, pleasant, gay festivities in which we can forget for a while the hardships of life and immerse ourselves in an atmosphere of music, dance, drinks, laughter, and a lot of cozy small-talk. But celebration in the Christian sense has very little to do with this. Celebration is only possible through the deep realization that life and death are never found completely separate.

Celebration can really come about only where fear and love, joy and sorrow, tears and smiles can exist together. Celebration is the acceptance of life in a constantly increasing awareness of its preciousness. And life is precious not only because it can be seen, touched, and tasted, but also because it will be gone one day.

When we celebrate a wedding, we celebrate a union as well as a departure, when we celebrate death we celebrate lost friendship as well as gained liberty. There can be tears after weddings and smiles after funerals. We can indeed make our sorrows, just as much as our joys, a part of our celebration of life in the deep realization that life and death are not opponents but do, in fact, kiss each other at every moment of our existence.

When we are born we become free to breathe on our own but lose the safety of our mother's body; when we go to school we are free to join a greater society but lose a particular place in our family; when we marry we find a new partner but lose the special tie we had with our parents; when we find work we win our independence by making our own money but lose the stimulation of teachers and fellow students; when we receive children we discover a new world but lose much of our freedom to move; when we are promoted we become more important in the eyes of others but lose the chance to take many risks; when we retire we finally have the chance to do what we wanted but lose the support of being wanted. When we have been able to celebrate life in all these decisive moments where gaining and losing — that is, life and death — touched each other all the time, we will be able to celebrate even our own dying because we have learned from life that he who loses it can find it (see Matt. 16:25).

— *Creative Ministry,* 91–92

DEATH AND RESURRECTION

Dying Like Jesus

We may be inclined to view the way Jesus prepared himself and his friends for his death as unique, far beyond any "normal" human way. But in fact, Jesus' way of dying offers us a hopeful example. We, too, can say to our friends, "It is for your own good that I am going, because if I go I can send the Spirit to you, and the Spirit will reveal to you the things to come...." Isn't "sending the Spirit" the best expression for not leaving those you love alone but offering them a new bond, deeper than the bond that existed in life? Doesn't "dying for others" mean dying so that others can continue to live, strengthened by the Spirit of our love?

Some people might protest, saying, "Jesus, the only Son of the Father, did send his Holy Spirit to us... but we are not Jesus, and we have no Holy Spirit to send!" But when we listen deeply to Jesus' words, we realize that we are called to live like him, to die like him, and to rise like him, because the Spirit — the divine love, which makes Jesus one with his Father — has been given to us. Not only the death of Jesus, but our death, too, is destined to be good for others. Not only the death of Jesus, but our death, too, is meant to bear fruit in other people's lives. Not only the death of Jesus, but our death, too, will bring the Spirit of God to those we leave behind. The great mystery is that all people who have lived with and in the Spirit of God participate through their deaths in the sending of the Spirit. Thus God's Spirit of love continues to be sent to us, and Jesus' death continues to bear fruit through all whose death is like his death, a death for others.

— *Our Greatest Gift*, 37–39

In Our Death, Our Oneness

People are dying every day, every hour, every minute. They die suddenly or slowly. They die on the streets of big cities or in comfortable homes. They die in isolation or surrounded by friends and family. They die in great pain or as if falling asleep. They die in anguish or in peace. But all of them die alone, facing the unknown.

Dying is indeed a reality of daily life. And yet, the world generally goes about its business disowning this reality. Dying is often a hidden event, something to ignore or deny....

Jesus was nailed to the cross, and for three hours he was dying. He died between two men. One of them said to the other: "We are paying for what we did. But this man has done nothing wrong" (Luke 23:41). Jesus lived his dying completely for others. The total exhaustion of his body, the abandonment by his friends, and even of his God, all became the gift of self. And as he hung dying in complete powerlessness, nailed against the wood of a tree, there was no bitterness, no desire for revenge, no resentment. Nothing to cling to. All to give.

"Unless a grain of wheat falls into the earth and dies, it remains only a single grain, but if it dies, it yields a rich harvest" (John 12:24). By being given away for others, his life became fruitful. Jesus, the completely innocent one, the one without sin, without guilt, without shame, died an excruciatingly painful death in order that death no longer would have to be ignored, but could become a gateway to life and the source of a new communion.

As we look at the dying Jesus, we see the dying world. Jesus, who on the cross drew all people to himself, died millions of deaths. He died not only the death of the rejected, the lonely, and the criminal, but also the death of the high and powerful, the famous and the popular. Most of all, he died the death of all the simple people who lived their ordinary lives and grew old and tired, and trusted that somehow their lives were not in vain.

We all must die. And we all will die alone. No one can make that final journey with us. We have to let go of what is most our own and trust that we did not live in vain. Somehow, dying is the greatest of all human moments because it is the moment in which we are asked to give everything. The way we die has not only much to do with the way *we* have lived, but also with the way that *those who come after* us will live.

Jesus' death reveals to us that we do not have to live pretending that death is not something that comes to all of us. As he hangs stretched out between heaven and earth, he asks us to look our mortality straight in the face and trust that death does not have the last word. We can then look at the dying in our world and give them hope; we can hold their dying bodies in our arms and trust that mightier arms than ours will receive them and give them the peace and joy they always desire.

In dying, all of humanity is one. And it was into this dying humanity that God entered so as to give us hope.

— *Walk with Jesus*, 69–71

Dying for Others

Why am I alive?...That question brings me to the heart of my vocation: to live with a burning desire to be with God and to be asked to keep proclaiming his love while missing its fulfillment.

Confronting death has helped me to understand better the tension that belongs to this vocation. Clearly, it is a tension not to be resolved but to be lived deeply enough to become fruitful. What I learned about dying is that I am called to die for others. The very simple truth is that the way in which I die affects many people. If I die with much anger and bitterness, I will leave my family and friends behind in confusion, guilt, shame, or weakness.

When I felt my death approaching [in a recent near-death experience], I suddenly realized how much I could influence the hearts of those whom I would leave behind. If I could truly say that I was grateful for what I had lived, eager to forgive and be forgiven, full of hope that those who loved me would continue their lives in joy and peace, and confident that Jesus who calls me would guide all who somehow had belonged to my life — if I could do that — I would, in the hour of my death, reveal more true spiritual freedom than I had been able to reveal during all the years of my life. I realized on a very deep level that dying is the most important act of living. It involves a choice to bind others with guilt or to set them free with gratitude....The dying have the unique opportunity to set free those whom they leave behind....

My deep desire to be united with God through Jesus did not spring from disdain for human relationships but from an acute awareness of the truth that dying in Christ can be, indeed, my greatest gift to others. In this perspective, life is a long journey of preparation — of preparing oneself to truly die for others. It is a series of little deaths in which we are asked to release many forms of clinging and to move increasingly from needing others to living for them. — *Beyond the Mirror,* 50–53

Let the Catcher Catch

The Flying Rodleighs are trapeze artists who perform in the German circus Simoneit-Barum. When the circus came to Freiburg two years ago, my friends Franz and Reny invited me and my father to see the show. I will never forget how enraptured I became when I first saw the Rodleighs move through the air, flying and catching as elegant dancers. The next day, I returned to the circus to see them again and introduced myself to them as one of their great fans. They invited me to attend their practice sessions, gave me free tickets, asked me to dinner, and suggested I travel with them for a week in the near future. I did, and we became good friends.

One day, I was sitting with Rodleigh, the leader of the troupe, in his caravan, talking about flying. He said, "As a flyer, I must have complete trust in my catcher. The public might think that I am the great star of the trapeze, but the real star is Joe, my catcher. He has to be there for me with split-second precision and grab me out of the air as I come to him in the long jump." "How does it work?" I asked. "The secret," Rodleigh said, "is that the flyer does nothing and the catcher does everything. When I fly to Joe, I have simply to stretch out my arms and hands and wait for him to catch me and pull me safely over the apron behind the catchbar."

"You do nothing!" I said, surprised. "Nothing," Rodleigh repeated. "The worst thing the flyer can do is to try to catch the catcher. I am not supposed to catch Joe. It's Joe's task to catch me. If I grabbed Joe's wrists, I might break them, or he might break mine, and that would be the end for both of us. A flyer must fly, and a catcher must catch, and the flyer must trust, with outstretched arms, that his catcher will be there for him."

When Rodleigh said this with so much conviction, the words of Jesus flashed through my mind: "Father into your hands I com-

mend my Spirit." Dying is trusting in the catcher. To care for the
dying is to say, "Don't be afraid. Remember that you are the beloved child of God. He will be there when you make your long
jump. Don't try to grab him; he will grab you. Just stretch out
your arms and hands and trust, trust, trust."

— *Our Greatest Gift,* 66–67

Living the Resurrection

On that morning of the first day of the week, Mary of Magdala
and Mary the mother of James and Salome found the tomb empty
and heard a young man in a white robe say: "He is not here."
Two of the disciples, Peter and John, entered the tomb and saw
the linen cloths lying on the ground and also the cloth that had
been over Jesus' head. Mary of Magdala heard him call her by
name, and Cleopas and his friend recognized him at Emmaus in
the breaking of the bread. In the evening of that same day, he
came and stood among his disciples, saying, "Peace be with you,"
and showed them his hands and his side.

As these things took place, new words broke out of the silence
of Holy Saturday and touched the hearts and the minds of the
men and women who had known and loved Jesus. These words
were: "He has risen, risen indeed." They were not shouted from
the rooftops or carried around the city on big placards. They
were whispered from ear to ear as an intimate message that could
be truly heard and understood only by a heart that had been
yearning for the coming of the Kingdom and had recognized its
first signs in the words and deeds of the man from Nazareth.

All is different and all is the same for those who say "Yes"
to the news that is whispered through the ages from one end of
the world to the other. Trees are still trees, rivers are still rivers,
mountains are still mountains, and people in their hearts are still
able to choose between love and fear. But all that has been lifted
up in the risen body of Jesus and placed at the right hand of God.
The prodigal child is placed in the loving embrace of the Father;
the little child is put in its mother's arms; the true heir has been
given the best robe and a precious ring, and brothers and sisters

invited to the same table. All is the same, and all is made new. As we live our lives with a resurrection faith, our burdens become light burdens and our yokes easy yokes because we have found rest in the gentle and humble heart of Jesus that belongs for all eternity to God. — *Walk with Jesus, 93–95*

A Prayer for Preparation

O Lord, when shall I die? I do not know and I hope it will not be soon. Not that I feel so attached to this life — I might be much more attached to it than I realize — but I feel so unprepared to face you I feel that by letting me live a little longer, you reveal your patience, you give me yet another chance to convert myself, you offer me more time to purify my heart. Time is your gift to me.

I remember how I felt ready to die five years ago, when I left the Abbey after a seven-month stay. Now I do not feel that way. I feel restless, not at peace, guilty, doubtful, and very dark. Let my time here be a time of change: a change to inner tranquillity, deep trust in your forgiveness and mercy, and complete surrender to you.

Thank you, Lord, for every day that you give me to come closer to you. Thank you for your patience and goodness. I pray that when I die I will be at peace. Hear my prayer. Amen.

— *A Cry for Mercy, 26*

3

Opening Our Hearts

※

This section highlights three spiritual qualities that characterize a converted or transformed follower of Jesus: intimacy, compassion, and gratefulness. Henri experienced God's love not as a moral teaching or abstract principle, but as something very intimate and delicate. We receive our belovedness in a very personal way, from a Thou who knows us intimately and continues to love us faithfully, even when we are behaving badly, self-rejecting, God-rejecting, or afraid. This personal presence of Jesus, speaking to us in our hearts, naturally calls us into intimacy with ourselves, and with those we love.

The closeness we seek with others mirrors the intimate presence that we have with God in solitude and "emptiness." Henri deepens this quality of "practicing belovedness" in the spiritual quality of compassion. But the practice of compassion is difficult, requiring us to transcend two difficult hurdles — the tendencies to pity and to judge others. These temptations are a rejection of intimacy and the antithesis of true friendship in Christ. Gratitude is, likewise, not a moral teaching, but a spontaneous response to the realization that we are the beloved. Still, even though gratitude arises spontaneously, it is also a discipline, a quality of presence to God, ourselves and others that must be consciously chosen and rechosen.

INTIMACY

Claiming Friendship

To know ourselves truly and acknowledge fully our own unique journey, we need to be known and acknowledged by others for who we are. We cannot live a spiritual life in secrecy. We cannot find our way to true freedom in isolation. Silence without speaking is as dangerous as solitude without community. They belong together.

Speaking about our cup and what it holds is not easy. It requires a true discipline because, just as we want to run from silence in order to avoid self-confrontation, we want to run from speaking about our inner life in order to avoid confrontation with others.

I am not suggesting that everyone we know or meet should hear about what is in our cup. To the contrary, it would be tactless, unwise, and even dangerous to expose our innermost being to people who cannot offer us safety and trust. That does not create community; it only causes mutual embarrassment and deepens our shame and guilt. But I do suggest that we need loving and caring friends with whom we can speak from the depth of our heart. Such friends can take away the paralysis that secrecy creates. They can offer us a safe and sacred place, where we can express our deepest sorrows and joys, and they can confront us in love, challenging us to a greater spiritual maturity.

We might object by saying: "I do not have such trustworthy friends, and I wouldn't know how to find them." But this objection comes from our fear of drinking the cup that Jesus asks us to drink.

When we are fully committed to the spiritual adventure of drinking our cup to the bottom, we will soon discover that people who are on the same journey will offer themselves to us for encouragement and friendship and love. It has been my own most blessed experience that God sends wonderful friends to those who make God their sole concern. This is the mysterious paradox Jesus speaks about when he says that when we leave those

who are close to us, for his sake and the sake of the Gospel, we
will receive a hundred times more in human support (see Mark
10:29–30).   — *Can You Drink the Cup?* 96–98

Revealing God's Faithfulness

To be truthful all human relationships must find their source in
God and witness to God's love. One of the most important qualities of God's love is faithfulness. God is a faithful God, a God
who fulfills the divine promise and will never let us down....
Through Jesus, God gives us the divine Spirit so that we can live
a God-like life. The Spirit is the breath of God. It is the intimacy
between Jesus and his Father. It is the divine communion. It is
God's love active within us.

This divine faithfulness is the core of our witness. By our
words, but most of all by our lives, we are to reveal God's faithfulness to the world. The world is not interested in faithfulness,
because faithfulness does not help in the acquisition of success,
popularity, and power. But when Jesus calls us to love one another as he has loved us, he calls us to faithful relationships,
not based on the pragmatic concerns of the world, but on the
knowledge of God's everlasting love.

Faithfulness, obviously, does not mean sticking it out together
to the bitter end. That is no reflection of God's love. Faithfulness
means that every decision we make in our lives together is guided
by the deep awareness that we are called to be living signs of
God's faithful presence among us. And this requires an attentiveness to one another that goes far beyond any formal obligation.
                                     — *Here and Now,* 128–29

A Family's Vocation

The gift of solitude makes the gift of intimacy possible. St. Paul
says: "Think of what is best for each other." When we live together in solitude — in reverence for God's loving Spirit — we can
then enter into real intimacy with each other; we can then not
only think but also do what is best for each other. When inti-

macy is born not out of solitude but out of a fearful loneliness, it quickly degenerates into a grasping, clinging possessiveness. . . .

When husband and wife expect from each other the fulfillment of their deepest need, they put inhuman claims on each other and develop a suffocating relationship. When parents use their children to gratify their unfulfilled needs for affection and sympathy, they imprison their children and prevent them from moving on to build their own unique lives. When you make your neighbor into a God, you make yourself into a demon.

But when intimacy is rooted in solitude, you can become persons to each other — persons in the sense of *personae,* which means sounding through. Then intimacy allows us to sound through a truth wider than we can grasp, a peace deeper than we can fathom, a love greater than we can contain. Then we become lovers who are not trying to fulfill each other but who want to sound through to each other the all-fulfilling love which embraces us all.

This has profound consequences for parents. Intimacy born out of solitude creates a space between marriage partners where real movement is possible, where a dance can take place. In their intimacy, the partners do not cling to each other, but move back and forth, near and far. This kind of intimacy allows for temporary silence, for moments of absence, for physical distance, for illness and weakness. But it also allows delightful joy, beautiful sensuality, full expression of body and mind, and moments of total surrender and blissful union. . . . In intimacy born of solitude, both ecstasy and agony have their place and deepen the creativity of life together.

But there is more. Intimacy born of solitude creates not only a space where partners can dance freely but also a space for others — especially children. The intimacy of marriage is the intimacy in which children can enter, grow, and develop, and from which they can depart without feelings of guilt. The intimacy of marriage allows the partners to see their own children as guests who enter into their home — guests who are received with excitement, wonderment, and expectation, guests who receive the freedom to discover their own talents and enjoy them, guests who are free to leave and continue their journey when they have the strength and the desire to do so. In intimacy born of solitude there is a mysterious space, wider and greater than we can imagine. It is a space where children, friends, and strangers can enter without fear, without need for rivalry or jealousy. It is a space where they can find their own solitude and listen to their own deepest self. Therefore, the great mystery of intimacy in the family is that it does not exclude others but rather includes them in that intimacy.

A mature family life is therefore a hospitable life. The mystery of love is that love creates space, not just for the immediate members of the family but for strangers as well. When a family is deprived of solitude and intimacy there is no space for strangers.... But when there is love, an unlimited space opens for others. The love between family members is greater than they themselves can contain. In their solitude and intimacy they evoke a love which transcends the limits of human togetherness; they evoke a divine love of which they have become visible witnesses. In this spacious divine love, which is revealed in the family, there is indeed room for strangers. In that love, strangers can become friends, yes, even members of the family. So we see how indeed the family can become the basis of the Christian community.

— "Spirituality and the Family," 10–12

COMPASSION

From Pity to Compassion

Compassion is something other than pity. Pity suggests distance, even a certain condescendence. I often act with pity. I give some money to a beggar on the streets of Toronto or New York City, but I do not look him in his eyes, sit down with him, or talk with him. I am too busy to really pay attention to the man who reaches out to me. My money replaces my personal attention and gives me an excuse to walk on.

Compassion means to become close to the one who suffers. But we can come close to another person only when we are willing to become vulnerable ourselves. A compassionate person says: "I am your brother; I am your sister; I am human, fragile, and mortal, just like you. I am not scandalized by your tears, nor afraid of your pain. I too have wept. I too have felt pain." We can be with the other only when the other ceases to be other and becomes like us.

This, perhaps, is the main reason that we sometimes find it easier to show pity than compassion. The suffering person calls us to become aware of our own suffering. How can I respond to someone's loneliness unless I am in touch with my own experience of loneliness? How can I be close to handicapped people when I refuse to acknowledge my own handicaps? How can I be with the poor when I am unwilling to confess my own poverty?

—*Here and Now,* 104–5

Giving Up Judgment

Imagine your having no need at all to judge anybody. Imagine your having no desire to decide whether someone is a good or bad person. Imagine your being completely free from the feeling that you have to make up your mind about the morality of someone's behavior. Imagine that you could say: "I am judging no one!"

Imagine — Wouldn't that be true inner freedom? The desert fathers from the fourth century said: "Judging others is a heavy burden." I have had a few moments in my life during which I felt free from all judgments about others. It felt as if a heavy burden had been taken away from me. At those moments I experienced an immense love for everyone I met, heard about, or read about. A deep solidarity with all people and a deep desire to love them broke down all my inner walls and made my heart as wide as the universe.

One such moment occurred after a seven-month stay in a Trappist monastery. I was so full of God's goodness that I saw that goodness wherever I went, even behind the facades of violence, destruction, and crime. I had to restrain myself from embracing the women and men who sold me groceries, flowers, and a new suit. They all seemed like saints to me!

We all have these moments if we are attentive to the movement of God's Spirit within us. They are like glimpses of heaven, glimpses of beauty and peace. It is easy to dismiss these moments as products of our dreams or poetic imagination. But when we choose to claim them as God's way of tapping us on our shoulders and showing us the deepest truth of our existence, we can gradually step beyond our need to judge others and our inclination to evaluate everybody and everything. Then we can grow toward real inner freedom and real sanctity.

— Here and Now, 60–63

Seeing Christ (a prayer)

You say to me, "What you have done to the least of mine, you have done to me." The hungry, the thirsty, the naked, the prisoners, the refugees, the lonely, the anguished, the dying, they are all around me and show me your broken heart. I see you every time I walk down the streets, every time I watch television or listen to the radio, every time I open a newspaper, every time I pay attention to a woman, a man, or a child who comes to me. I see you every time I let my eyes see the pain of all those with whom I live day after day. You are so close, closer than I ever knew before I looked at your pierced side. You are in my house, on my street, in my town, in my country. You are where I walk and where I sit, where I sleep and where I eat, where I work and where I play. You are never far from me.

Oh Lord Jesus, this is not a sentimental thought. Oh no . . . You who drew all people to yourself as you were lifted up in your pain and in your glory, you stay with us as the wounded and risen Lord. Whenever I touch your broken heart, I touch the hearts of your broken people, and whenever I touch the hearts of your broken people, I touch your heart.

— Heart Speaks to Heart, 53–54

Becoming World

Often I have said to people, "I will pray for you," but how often did I really enter into the full reality of what that means? I now see how indeed I can enter deeply into the other and pray to God from his center. When I really bring my friends and the many I pray for into my innermost being and feel their pains, their struggles, their cries in my own soul, then I leave myself, so to speak, and become them, then I have compassion. Compassion lies at the heart of our prayer for our fellow human beings. When I pray for the world, I become the world; when I pray for the endless needs of the millions, my soul expands and wants to embrace them all and bring them into the presence of God.

But in the midst of that experience I realize that compassion is not mine but God's gift to me. I cannot embrace the world, but God can. I cannot pray, but God can pray in me. When God became as we are, that is, when God allowed all of us to enter into his intimate life, it became possible for us to share in his infinite compassion.

In praying for others, I lose myself and become the other, only to be found by the divine love which holds the whole of humanity in a compassionate embrace.   —*Genesee Diary*, 123

The Way of the Dalai Lama

I know of few people who have seen as much suffering as the Dalai Lama. As the spiritual and political leader of Tibet he was driven from his own country and witnessed the systematic killing, torture, oppression, and expulsion of his people. Still, I know of few people who radiate so much peace and joy.

The Dalai Lama's generous and disarming laughter is free from any hatred or bitterness toward the Chinese who ravaged his land and murdered his people. He says: "They too are human beings who struggle to find happiness and deserve our compassion."

How is it possible that a man who has been subjected to such persecution is not filled with anger and a desire for revenge? When asked that question the Dalai Lama explains how, in his meditation, he allows all the suffering of his people and their oppressors to enter into the depth of his heart, and there to be transformed into compassion.

What a spiritual challenge! While I anxiously wonder how to help the people in Bosnia, South Africa, Guatemala, and, yes, Tibet...the Dalai Lama calls me to gather all the suffering of the people of this world in the center of my being and to become there the raw material for my compassionate love.

Isn't that, too, the way of Jesus? Shortly before his death and resurrection, Jesus said: "When I am lifted up from the earth, I shall draw all people to myself." Jesus took upon himself the suffering of all people and made it into a gift of compassion to his Father. That, indeed, is the way for us to follow.

— Here and Now, 47–48

My House Is Yours

Once we have found the center of our life in our own heart and have accepted our aloneness, not as a fate but as a vocation, we are able to offer freedom to others. Once we have given up our desire to be fully fulfilled, we can offer emptiness to others. Once we have become poor, we can be a good host. It is indeed the paradox of hospitality that poverty makes a good host. Poverty is the inner disposition that allows us to take away our defenses and convert our enemies into friends. We can perceive the stranger as an enemy only as long as we have something to defend. But when we say, "Please enter. My house is your house, my joy is your joy, my sadness is your sadness, and my life is your life," we have nothing to defend, since we have nothing to lose but all to give.

Turning the other cheek means showing our enemies that they can be our enemies only while supposing that we are anxiously clinging to our private property, whatever it is: our knowledge, our good name, our land, our money, or the many objects we have collected around us. But who will be our robber when everything he wants to steal from us becomes our gift to him? Who can lie to us, when only the truth will serve him well? Who wants to sneak into our back door, when our front door is wide open?

Poverty makes a good host.   *— Reaching Out,* 73

GRATITUDE

All Is Grace

"We are really grateful for all the good things.... We simply have to accept or try to forget the painful moments." The attitude expressed in these words made me aware of how often we tend to divide our past into good things to remember with gratitude and painful things to accept or forget. Once we accept this division, however, we quickly develop a mentality in which we hope to collect more good memories than bad memories, more things to be grateful for than things to be resentful about, more things to celebrate than things to complain about. But this way of thinking, which at first glance seems quite natural, prevents us from truly allowing our whole past to be the source from which we live our future. Is this the gratitude to which the Gospel calls us?...

Gratitude is not a simple emotion or an obvious attitude. It is a difficult discipline to constantly reclaim my whole past as the concrete way in which God has led me to this moment and is sending me into the future. It is hard precisely because it challenges me to face the painful moments — experiences of rejection and abandonment, feelings of loss and failure — and gradually to discover in them the pruning hands of God purifying my heart for deeper love, stronger hope, and broader faith. Jesus says to his disciples that although they are as intimately related to him as branches are to the vine, they still need to be pruned in order to bear more fruit (John 15:1–5). Pruning means cutting, reshaping, removing what diminishes vitality....

Grateful people are those who can celebrate even the pains of life because they trust that when harvest time comes the fruit will show that the pruning was not punishment but purification.

I am gradually learning that the call to gratitude asks us to say "everything is grace." When our gratitude for the past is only partial, our hope for a new future can never be full.... If we are to be truly ready for a new task in the service of God, truly joyful at the prospect of a new vocation, truly free to be sent into a new mission, our entire past, gathered into the spaciousness of a converted heart, must become the source of energy that moves us toward the future.   — "All Is Grace," 39–41

Fecundity

Gratitude flows from the recognition that all that is, is a divine gift born out of love and freely given to us so that we may offer thanks and share it with others.

The more we touch the intimate love of God which creates, sustains, and guides us, the more we recognize the multitude of fruits that come forth from that love. They are fruits of the Spirit, such as: joy, peace, kindness, goodness, and gentleness. When we encounter any of these fruits, we always experience them as gifts.

When, for instance, we enjoy a good atmosphere in the family, a peaceful mood among friends, or a spirit of cooperation and mutual support in the community, we intuitively know that we did not produce it. It cannot be made, imitated, or exported. To people who are jealous and who would like to have our joy and peace, we cannot give a formula to produce it or a method to acquire it. It is always perceived as a gift, to which the only appropriate response is gratitude.

Every time we experience real goodness or gentleness we know it is a gift. If we say: "Well, she gets paid to be nice to us," or "He only says such friendly things because he wants something from us," we can no longer receive that goodness as a gift. We grow from receiving and giving gifts.

Life loses its dynamism and exuberance when everything that happens to us is viewed as a predictable result of predictable actions. It degenerates into commerce, a continuous buying and selling of goods, whether physical, emotional, or spiritual goods. Without a spirit of gratitude, life flattens out and becomes dull and boring. But when we continue to be surprised by new manifestations of life and continue to praise and thank God and our neighbor, routine and boredom cannot take hold. Then all of life becomes a reason for saying thanks. Thus, fecundity and gratitude can never be separated.   — Lifesigns, 70–71

A Discipline

In the past I always thought of gratitude as a spontaneous response to the awareness of gifts received, but now I realize that gratitude can also be lived as a discipline. The discipline of gratitude is the explicit effort to acknowledge that all I am and have is given to me as a gift of love, a gift to be celebrated with joy.

Gratitude as a discipline involves a conscious choice. I can choose to be grateful even when my emotions and feelings are still steeped in hurt and resentment. It is amazing how many occasions present themselves in which I can choose gratitude instead of a complaint. I can choose to be grateful when I am criticized, even when my heart still responds in bitterness. I can choose to speak about goodness and beauty, even when my inner eye still looks for someone to accuse or something to call ugly. I can choose to listen to the voices that forgive and to look at the faces that smile, even while I still hear words of revenge and see grimaces of hatred.

There is always the choice between resentment and gratitude because God has appeared in my darkness, urged me to come home, and declared in a voice filled with affection: "You are with me always, and all I have is yours." Indeed, I can choose to dwell in the darkness in which I stand, point to those who are seemingly better off than I, lament about the many misfortunes that have plagued me in the past, and thereby wrap myself up in my resentment. But I don't have to do this. There is the option to look into the eyes of the one who came out to search for me and see therein that all I am and all I have is pure gift calling for gratitude.

The choice for gratitude rarely comes without some real effort. But each time I make it, the next choice is a little easier, a little freer, a little less self-conscious. Because every gift I acknowledge reveals another and another until finally, even the most normal, obvious, and seemingly mundane event or encounter proves to be filled with grace. There is an Estonian proverb that says: "Who does not thank for little will not thank for much." Acts of gratitude make one grateful because, step by step, they reveal that all is grace.   *—The Return of the Prodigal Son,* 80

4

God's Presence and Absence

This section searches Henri's writings for clues as to why the manifestations of God — as Father, as Christ, and as Holy Spirit — are sometimes vivid and sometimes elusive, even absent. What are we to make of these seeming appearances and disappearances?

We begin with an exploration of Henri's faith that Jesus' story is also our story. In this way, the reality of Jesus is as tangible as our own lives. Throughout his ministry, Henri rejected the idea that Jesus wanted to set himself apart as a special, perfect person to admire and idealize. Rather, Jesus' belovedness in God is ours, his Spirit-filled community is ours, and his trial by fire is ours as well. Moreover, God speaks through us as God spoke through Jesus, through the power of the Holy Spirit, and gives us the same eternal life. God is with us in every dimension of our lives, even in our fear. God is revealed to us through Scripture, music, prayer, intimate friendship, and in nature. And sometimes our lives are transformed in such startling and graced ways that we know, through faith, God is very near.

But Henri's writings also witness to God's apparent absence. Even though Jesus' story illuminates our story and reveals our true self, God transcends us and is mystery to us. We can never grasp God fully nor perceive God directly.

Sometimes, as in Henri's life, we search for Christ and cannot find him. In his emphasis on the rhythm of Christ's absence and presence, Henri carries on an ancient Christian understanding rooted in Hebrew Scripture, especially the Song of Songs. In this book, our souls are the bride longing for God, our bridegroom. We have glimpsed the deep, satisfying experience of complete union with the beloved. Often, when the beloved knocks, we go to the door filled with hope, love, and expectation, only to find that the beloved has just left or taken another form. Christian theologians have often referred to these two distinct experiences in faith as kataphatic (through images) and apophatic (without images), and different Christian theologians have recommended one of these approaches to God over the other. Henri's experience is a balance of the two. In giving ourselves to God we "let go and let God," without knowing for sure ahead of time how, or even if, God's loving presence will be experienced. No one can control or completely know God. True holiness, like the wind, blows where it will, and the Christian journey is like a dance that weaves in and out of these two dimensions of tangible reality and mystery.

JESUS' STORY IS OUR STORY

Being Like Jesus

Our lives are destined to become like the life of Jesus. The whole purpose of Jesus' ministry is to bring us to the house of his Father. Not only did Jesus come to free us from the bonds of sin and death, he also came to lead us into the intimacy of his divine life. It is difficult for us to imagine what this means. We tend to emphasize the distance between Jesus and ourselves. We see Jesus as the all-knowing and all-powerful Son of God who is unreachable for us sinful, broken human beings. But in thinking this way, we forget that Jesus came to give us his own life. He came to lift us up into loving community with the Father. Only when we recognize the radical purpose of Jesus' ministry will we be able to understand the meaning of the spiritual life. Everything that be-

longs to Jesus is given for us to receive. All that Jesus does we
may also do.   — *Making All Things New*, 50–51

Living from Belovedness

When Jesus was baptized in the Jordan, he heard a voice from
heaven, saying, "This is my beloved Son, with whom I am well
pleased" (Matt. 3:17). These words revealed the true identity of
Jesus as the beloved....I know now that the words spoken to
Jesus when he was baptized are words spoken also to me and to
all who are brothers and sisters of Jesus.

My tendencies toward self-rejection and self-depreciation
make it hard to hear these words truly and let them descend into
the center of my heart. But once I have received these words fully,
I am set free from my compulsion to prove myself to the world
and can live in it without belonging to it. Once I have accepted
the truth that I am God's beloved child, unconditionally loved, I
can be sent into the world to speak and to act as Jesus did.

The great spiritual task facing me is to so fully trust that I
belong to God that I can be free in the world — free to speak
even when my words are not received; free to act even when my
actions are criticized, ridiculed, or considered useless; free also to
receive love from people and to be grateful for all the signs of
God's presence in the world. I am convinced that I will truly be
able to love the world when I fully believe that I am loved far
beyond its boundaries.   — *Beyond the Mirror*, 56–58

The Holy Spirit in Us

[Jesus] became like us so that we might become like him. He did
not cling to his equality with God, but emptied himself and became as we are so that we might become like him and thus share
in his divine life.

This radical transformation of our lives is the work of the Holy
Spirit. The disciples could hardly comprehend what Jesus meant.
As long as Jesus was present to them in the flesh, they did not yet

recognize his full presence in the Spirit. That is why Jesus said: "It is for your own good that I am going because unless I go, the Advocate [the Holy Spirit] will not come to you; but if I do go, I will send him to you" (John 16:7)....

Thus Pentecost is the completion of Jesus' mission. On Pentecost the fullness of Jesus' ministry becomes visible. When the Holy Spirit descends upon the disciples and dwells with them, their lives are transformed into Christlike lives, lives shaped by the same love that exists between the Father and Son. The spiritual life is indeed a life in which we are lifted up to become partakers of the divine life.

To be lifted up into the divine life of the Father, the Son, and the Holy Spirit does not mean, however, to be taken out of the world. On the contrary, those who have entered into the spiritual life are precisely the ones who are sent into the world to continue and fulfill the work that Jesus began. The spiritual life does not remove us from the world but leads us deeper into it. Jesus says to his Father, "As you sent me into the world, I have sent them into the world" (John 17:18). He makes it clear that precisely because his disciples no longer belong to the world, they can live in the world as he did.

— Making All Things New, 52–55

A Communion of Likeness

Communion with Jesus means becoming like him. With him we are nailed on the cross, with him we are laid in the tomb, with him we are raised up to accompany lost travelers on their journey. Communion, becoming Christ, leads us to a new realm of being. It ushers us into the Kingdom. There the old distinctions between happiness and sadness, success and failure, praise and blame, health and sickness, life and death, no longer exist. There we no longer belong to the world that keeps dividing, judging, separating, and evaluating. There we belong to Christ and Christ to us, and with Christ we belong to God.

— With Burning Hearts, 74–75

GOD WITH US

One of Us

The truly good news is that God is not a distant God, a God
to be feared and avoided, a God of revenge, but a God who is
moved by our pains and participates in the fullness of the human
struggle....

God is a compassionate God. This means, first of all, that he
is a God who has chosen to be God-with-us.... As soon as we
call God "God-with-us," we enter into a new relationship of intimacy with him. By calling him Immanuel, we recognize that he
has committed himself to live in solidarity with us, to share our
joys and pains, to defend and protect us, and to suffer all of life
with us. The God-with-us is a close God, a God whom we call
our refuge, our stronghold, our wisdom, and even, more intimately, our helper, our shepherd, our love. We will never really
know God as a compassionate God if we do not understand with
our heart and mind that "he lived among us" (John 1:14).

— *Compassion*, 18, 13, 15

Do Not Be Afraid

Though we think of ourselves as followers of Jesus, we are often
seduced by the fearful questions the world presents to us. Without fully realizing it, we become anxious, nervous, worrying
people caught in the questions of survival: our own survival, the
survival of our families, friends, and colleagues, the survival of
our church, our country, and our world. Once these fearful survival questions become the guiding questions of our lives, we tend
to dismiss words spoken from the house of love as unrealistic,
romantic, sentimental, pious, or just useless. When love is offered
as an alternative to fear we say: "Yes, yes, that sounds beautiful,
but...."

The "but" reveals how much we live in the grip of the world,
a world which calls Christians naive and raises "realistic" questions: "Yes, but what if you grow old and there is nobody to help

you? Yes, but what if you lose your job and you have no money to take care of yourself and your family? Yes, but what if refugees come to this country by the millions and disrupt the ways we have been living for so long? Yes, but what if the Cubans and Russians become powerful in Central America and start building their missiles in our own backyard? . . . "

Are we so accustomed to living in fear that we have become deaf to the voice that says: "Do not be afraid." This reassuring voice, which repeats over and over again: "Do not be afraid, have no fear," is the voice we most need to hear. This voice was heard by Zechariah when Gabriel, the angel of the Lord, appeared to him in the temple and told him that his wife, Elizabeth, would bear a son; this voice was heard by Mary when the same angel entered her house in Nazareth and announced that she would conceive, bear a child, and name him Jesus; this voice was also heard by the women who came to the tomb and saw that the stone was rolled away. "Do not be afraid, do not be afraid, do not be afraid." The voice uttering these words sounds all through history as the voice of God's messengers, be they angels or saints. It is the voice that announces a whole new way of being, a being in the house of love, the house of the Lord.

Why is there no reason to fear any longer? Jesus himself answers this question succinctly when he approaches his frightened disciples walking on the lake: "It is I. Do not be afraid" (John 6:21). The house of love is the house of Christ, the place where we can think, speak, and act in the way of God — not in the way of a fear-filled world. — *Lifesigns,* 19–21

Angels' Wings

Gradually I am becoming aware of a new dimension in my prayer life. It is hard to find words for it, but it feels like a protective presence of God, Mary, the angels, and the saints that exists in the midst of distractions, fears, temptations, and inner confusion.

While my prayers were not at all intensive or profound, I had a real desire to spend time in prayer this week. I enjoyed just sitting in the small dark side chapel of the mother house of the Vincentian Sisters. I felt surrounded by goodness, gentleness, kindness, and acceptance. I felt as if angels' wings were keeping me safe: a protective cloud covering me and keeping me there. Though it is very hard to express, this new experience is the experience of being protected against the dangers of a seductive world.

But this protection is very soft, gentle, caring. Not the protection of a wall or a metal screen. It is more like a hand on my shoulder or a kiss on my forehead. But for all this protection, I am not taken away from the dangers. I am not lifted from the seductive world. I am not removed from violence, hatred, lust, and greed. In fact, I feel them in the center of my being, screaming for my full attention. They are restless and noisy. Still, this hand, these lips, these eyes are present and I know that I am safe, held in love, cared for, and protected by the good spirits of heaven.

So I am praying while not knowing how to pray. I am resting while feeling restless, at peace while tempted, safe while still anxious, surrounded by a cloud of light while still in darkness, in love while still doubting.   — *The Road to Daybreak,* 133–34

The Eyes of Christ

To see Christ is to see God and all of humanity. This mystery has evoked in me a burning desire to see the face of Jesus. Countless images have been created over the centuries to portray the face of Jesus. Some have helped me to see his face; others have not. But when I saw Andrew Rublev's icon of Christ, I saw what I had never seen before and felt what I had never felt before. I knew immediately that my eyes had been blessed in a very special way.

Andrew Rublev painted his icon of Christ at the beginning of the fifteenth century as part of a tier of icons he made for a church in the Russian city of Zvenigorod. Hence, the icon is often called the 'Savior of Zvenigorod.' . . .

This face-to-face experience leads us to the heart of the great mystery of the incarnation. We can see God and live! As we try to fix our eyes on the eyes of Jesus we know that we are seeing the eyes of God. What greater desire is there in the human heart than to see God? With the apostle Philip our hearts cry out: "Lord, let

us see the Father and then we shall be satisfied." And the Lord
answers:

> To have seen me is to have seen the Father.
> Do you not believe
> that I am in the Father
> and the Father is in me? (John 14:8–10)

Jesus is the full revelation of God, "the image of the unseen
God" (Col. 1:15). Looking into the eyes of Jesus is the fulfillment
of our deepest aspiration....

It is hard to grasp this mystery, but we must try to sense how
the eyes of the Word incarnate truly embrace in their gaze all
there is to be seen. The eyes of Rublev's Christ are the eyes of the
Son of Man and the Son of God described in the book of Revelation. They are like flames of fire which penetrate the mystery
of the divine. They are the eyes of one whose face is like the sun
shining with all its force, and who is known by the name: Word
of God (see Rev. 1:14, 2:18, 1:16, 19:12–13). They are the eyes
of the one who is "Light from Light, true God from true God, be-
gotten, not made, one in being with the Father...through whom
all things were made" (Nicene Creed). He is indeed the light in
whom all is created. He is the light of the first day when God
spoke the light, divided it from the darkness, and saw that it was
good (Gen. 1:3). He is also the light of the new day shining in the
dark, a light that darkness could not overpower (John 1:5). He is
the true light that enlightens all people (John 1:9). It is awesome
to look into the eyes of the only one who truly sees the light, and
whose seeing is not different from his being....

The one who sees unceasingly the limitless goodness of God
came to the world, saw it broken to pieces by human sin, and was
moved to compassion. The same eyes which see into the heart
of God saw the suffering hearts of God's people and wept (see
John 11:36). These eyes, which burn like flames of fire penetrating God's own interiority, also hold oceans of tears for the human
sorrow of all times and all places. That is the secret of the eyes
of Andrew Rublev's Christ.

—Behold the Beauty of the Lord, 45, 54–56

To See and Be Seen (a prayer)

Lord Jesus, I look at you, and my eyes are fixed on your eyes.
Your eyes penetrate the eternal mystery of the divine and see the
glory of God. They are also the eyes that saw Simon, Andrew,
Nathanael, and Levi, the eyes that saw the woman with a hem-
orrhage, the widow of Nain, the blind, the lame, the lepers, and
the hungry crowd, the eyes that saw the sad, rich ruler, the fearful disciples on the lake, and the sorrowful women at the tomb.
Your eyes, O Lord, see in one glance the inexhaustible love of
God and the seemingly endless agony of all people who have lost
faith in that love and are like sheep without a shepherd. As I look
into your eyes, they frighten me because they pierce like flames
of fire my innermost being, but they console me as well, because
these flames are purifying and healing. Your eyes are so severe yet
so loving, so unmasking yet so protecting, so penetrating yet so
caressing, so profound yet so intimate, so distant yet so inviting.

I gradually realize that I want to be seen by you, to dwell under
your caring gaze, and to grow strong and gentle in your sight.
Lord, let me see what you see — the love of God and the suffering
of people — so that my eyes may become more and more like
yours, eyes that can heal wounded hearts.

— *The Road to Daybreak, 56*

God Is Looking for Me

For most of my life I have struggled to find God, to know God,
to love God. I have tried hard to follow the guidelines of the spiritual life — pray always, work for others, read the Scriptures —
and to avoid the many temptations to dissipate myself. I have
failed many times but always tried again, even when I was close
to despair.

Now I wonder whether I have sufficiently realized that during all this time God has been trying to find me, to know me,
and to love me. The question is not "How am I to find God?"
but "How am I to let myself be found by him?" The question
is not "How am I to know God?" but "How am I to let myself

be known by God?" And, finally, the question is not "How am I to love God?" but "How am I to let myself be loved by God?" God is looking into the distance for me, trying to find me, and longing to bring me home. In all three parables which Jesus tells in response to the question of why he eats with sinners, he puts the emphasis on God's initiative. God is the shepherd who goes looking for his lost sheep. God is the woman who lights a lamp, sweeps out the house, and searches everywhere for her lost coin until she has found it. God is the father who watches and waits for his children, runs out to meet them, embraces them, pleads with them, begs and urges them to come home.

It might sound strange, but God wants to find me as much as, if not more than, I want to find God. Yes, God needs me as much as I need God. God is not the patriarch who stays home, doesn't move, and expects his children to come to him, apologize for their aberrant behavior, beg for forgiveness, and promise to do better. To the contrary, he leaves the house, ignoring his dignity by running toward them, pays no heed to apologies and promises of change, and brings them to the table richly prepared for them.

I am beginning now to see how radically the character of my spiritual journey will change when I no longer think of God as hiding out and making it as difficult as possible for me to find him, but, instead, as the one who is looking for me while I am doing the hiding.

— The Return of the Prodigal Son, 100–101

God, Our Mother

Every time I look at the tent-like and wings-like cloak in Rembrandt's painting, I sense the motherly quality of God's love and my heart begins to sing in words inspired by the Psalmist:

> You who dwell in the shelter of the Most High
> and abide in the shade of the Almighty — say to your God:
> "My refuge, my stronghold, my God in whom I trust!
>
> ... You conceal me with your pinions
> and under your wings I shall find refuge."

And so, under the aspect of an old Jewish patriarch, there emerges also a motherly God receiving her son home.

As I now look again at Rembrandt's old man bending over his returning son and touching his shoulders with his hands, I begin to see not only a father who "clasps his son in his arms," but also a mother who caresses her child, surrounds him with the warmth of her body, and holds him against the womb from which he sprang. Thus the "return of the prodigal son" becomes the return to God's womb, the return to the very origins of being, and again echoes Jesus' exhortation to Nicodemus, to be reborn from above.

Now I understand better also the enormous stillness of this portrait of God. There is no sentimentality here, no romanticism, no simplistic tale with a happy ending. What I see here is God as mother, receiving back into her womb the one whom she made in her own image. The near-blind eyes, the hands, the cloak, the bent-over body, they all call forth the divine maternal love, marked by grief, desire, hope, and endless waiting.

The mystery, indeed, is that God in her infinite compassion has linked herself for eternity with the life of her children. She has freely chosen to become dependent on her creatures, whom she has gifted with freedom. This choice causes her grief when they leave; this choice brings her gladness when they return. But her joy will not be complete until all who have received life from her have returned home and gather together around the table prepared for them.

The parable of the prodigal son is a story that speaks about a love that existed before any rejection was possible and that will still be there after all rejections have taken place. It is the first and everlasting love of a God who is Father as well as Mother.

— "The Vulnerable God," 34–35

To Jesus (a prayer)

Dear Lord, help me keep my eyes on you. You are the incarnation of divine love, you are the expression of God's infinite compassion, you are the visible manifestation of God's holiness. You are beauty, goodness, gentleness, forgiveness, and mercy. In you all can be found. Outside of you nothing can be found. Why should I look elsewhere or go elsewhere? You have the words of eternal life, you are food and drink, you are the Way, the Truth, and the Life. You are the light that shines in the darkness, the lamp on the lampstand, the house on the hilltop. You are the perfect Icon of God. In and through you I can see the Heavenly Father, and with you I can find my way to him. O Holy One, Beautiful One, Glorious One, be my Lord, my Savior, my Redeemer, my Guide, my Consoler, my Comforter, my Hope, my Joy and my Peace. To you I want to give all that I am. Let me be generous, not stingy or hesitant. Let me give you all — all I have, think, do, and feel. It is yours, O Lord. Please accept it and make it fully your own. Amen.   — *A Cry for Mercy,* 34

A HIDDEN GOD

Presence in Absence

God is "beyond," beyond our heart and mind, beyond our feelings and thoughts, beyond our expectations and desires, and beyond all the events and experiences that make up our life. Still he is in the center of all of it. Here we touch the heart of prayer since here it becomes manifest that in prayer the distinction between God's presence and God's absence no longer really distinguishes. In prayer, God's presence is never separated from his absence and God's absence is never separated from his presence. His presence is so much beyond the human experience of being together that it quite easily is perceived as absence. His absence, on the other hand, is often so deeply felt that it leads to a new sense of his presence. This is powerfully expressed in Psalm 22:1–5:

> My God, my God, why have you deserted me?
> How far from saving me, the words I groan!
> I call all day, my God, but you never answer,
> all night long I call and cannot rest.

Yet, Holy One, you who make your home in the praises of
    Israel,
in you our fathers put their trust,
they trusted and you rescued them;
they called to you for help and they were saved,
they never trusted you in vain.

This prayer not only is the expression of the experience of the
people of Israel, but also the culmination of the Christian experience. When Jesus spoke these words on the cross, total aloneness
and full acceptance touched each other. In that moment of complete emptiness all was fulfilled. In that hour of darkness new
light was seen. While death was witnessed, life was affirmed.
Where God's absence was most loudly expressed, his presence
was most profoundly revealed. When God himself in his humanity became part of our most painful experience of God's absence,
he became most present to us. It is in this mystery that we enter
when we pray.   — *Reaching Out,* 90–91

Mystery to Mystery

Our lives vibrate between two darknesses. We hesitantly come
forth out of the darkness of birth and slowly vanish into the
darkness of death. We move from dust to dust, from unknown
to unknown, from mystery to mystery.

We try to keep a vital balance on the thin rope that is stretched
between two definitive endings we have never seen or understood.
We are surrounded by the reality of the unseen, which fills every
part of our life with a moment of terror but at the same time
holds the secret mystery of our being alive.

— *Creative Ministry,* 90–91

Jesus, the Hidden God

Jesus is the hidden God. He became a human being among a
small, oppressed people, under very difficult circumstances. He

was held in contempt by the rulers of his country and was put to a shameful death between two criminals.

There was nothing spectacular about Jesus' life. Far from it! Even when you look at Jesus' miracles, you find that he did not heal or revive people in order to get publicity. He frequently forbade them even to talk about it. His resurrection too was a hidden event. Only his disciples and a few of the women and men who had known him intimately before his death saw him as the risen Lord.

Now that Christianity has become one of the major world religions and millions of people utter the name of Jesus every day, it's hard for us to believe that Jesus revealed God in hiddenness. But neither Jesus' life nor his death nor his resurrection were intended to astound us with the great power of God. God became a lowly, hidden, almost invisible God.

I'm constantly struck by the fact that wherever the Gospel of Jesus bears fruit, we come across this hiddenness. The great Christians throughout history have always been lowly people who sought to be hidden. Benedict hid himself in the vale of Subiaco, Francis in the Carceri outside Assisi, Ignatius in the grotto of Manresa, the little Thérèse in the Carmel of Lisieux. Whenever you hear about saintly people, you sense a deep longing for that hiddenness, that seclusion. We so easily forget it, but Paul too withdrew into the wilderness for two years before he started on his preaching mission....

Many great minds and spirits have lost their creative force through too early or too rapid exposure to the public. We know it; we sense it; but we easily forget it because our world persists in proclaiming the big lie: "Being unknown means being unloved." If you're ready to trust your intuition and so preserve a degree of healthy skepticism in the face of the current propaganda, you are more likely to detect the hidden presence of God....

Now look at Jesus who came to reveal God to us, and you see that popularity in any form is the very thing he avoids. He is constantly pointing out that God reveals himself in secrecy. It sounds very paradoxical, but accepting and, I would venture to say, entering into that paradox sets you on the road of the spiritual life.
— *Letters to Marc,* 65–68

The Hidden Resurrection

The world didn't notice Jesus' resurrection; only a few knew, those to whom Jesus had chosen to show himself and whom he wanted to send out to announce God's love to the world just as he had done.

The hiddenness of Jesus' resurrection is important to me. Although the resurrection of Jesus is the cornerstone of my faith, it is not something to use as an argument, nor is it something to use to reassure people. It somehow doesn't take death seriously enough to say to a dying person, "Don't be afraid. After your death you will be resurrected as Jesus was, meet all your friends again, and be forever happy in the presence of God." This suggests that after death everything will be basically the same, except that our troubles will be gone. Nor does it take seriously Jesus himself, who did not live through his own death as if it were little else than a necessary passage to a better life. Finally, it doesn't take seriously the dying, who, like us, know nothing about what is beyond this time-and-place-bound existence.

The resurrection does not solve our problems about dying and death. It is not the happy ending to our life's struggle, nor is it the big surprise that God has kept in store for us. No, the resurrection is the expression of God's faithfulness to Jesus and to all God's children.... [It] is God's way of revealing to us that nothing that belongs to God will ever go to waste. What belongs to God will never get lost — not even our mortal bodies. The resurrection doesn't answer any of our curious questions about life after death, such as, How will it be? How will it look? But it does reveal to us that, indeed, love is stronger than death. After that revelation, we must remain silent, leave the whys, wheres, hows, and whens behind, and simply trust.

— *Our Greatest Gift,* 108–9

Purifying Absence

The mystery of God's presence can be touched only by a deep awareness of his absence. It is in the center of our longing for the absent God that we discover his footprints and realize that our desire to love God is born out of the love with which he has touched us. In the patient waiting for the loved one, we discover how much he has filled our lives already. Just as the love of a mother for her son can grow deeper when he is far away, just as children can learn to appreciate their parents more when they have left the home, just as lovers can rediscover each other during long periods of absence, so our intimate relationship with God can become deeper and more mature by the purifying experience of his absence. By listening to our longings, we hear God as their creator. By touching the center of our solitude, we sense that we have been touched by loving hands. By watching carefully our endless desire to love, we come to the growing awareness that we can love only because we have been loved first, and that we can offer intimacy only because we are born out of the inner intimacy of God himself.

In our violent times, in which destruction of life is so rampant and the raw wounds of humanity so visible, it is very hard to tolerate the experience of God as a purifying absence and to keep our hearts open so as to patiently and reverently prepare his way. We are tempted to grasp rapid solutions instead of inquiring about the validity of the questions. Our inclination to put faith in any suggestion that promises quick healing is so great that it is not surprising that spiritual experiences are mushrooming all over the place and have become highly sought after commercial items. Many people flock to places and persons who promise intensive experiences of togetherness, cathartic emotions of exhilaration and sweetness, and liberating sensations of rapture and ecstasy. In our desperate need for fulfillment and our restless search for the experience of divine intimacy, we are all too prone to construct our own spiritual events. In our impatient culture, it has indeed become extremely difficult to see much salvation in waiting.

But...the God who saves is not made by human hands. He transcends our psychological distinctions between "already" and "not yet," absence and presence, leaving and returning.

— *Reaching Out*, 128–30

God beyond Thought

God cannot be understood; he cannot be grasped by the human mind. The truth escapes our human capacities. The only way to come close to it is by a constant emphasis on the limitations of our human capacities to "have" or "hold" the truth. We can neither explain God nor his presence in history. As soon as we identify God with any specific event or situation, we play God and distort the truth. We can be faithful only in our affirmation that God has not deserted us but calls us in the middle of all the unexplainable absurdities of life. It is very important to be deeply aware of this. There is a great and subtle temptation to suggest to myself or others where God is working and where not, when he is present and when not, but nobody, no Christian, no priest, no monk, has any "special" knowledge about God. God cannot be limited by any human concept or prediction. He is greater than our mind and heart and perfectly free to reveal himself where and when he wants.   — *Genesee Diary,* 108–9, 116–17

A Hidden Hour of Prayer (in Bolivia)

Every morning at 6:45 I go to the small convent of the Carmelite Sisters for an hour of prayer and meditation. I say "every morning," but there are exceptions. Fatigue, busyness, and pre-occupations often serve as arguments for not going. Yet without this one hour a day for God, my life loses its coherency and I start experiencing my days as a series of random incidents and accidents.

My hour in the Carmelite chapel is more important than I can fully know myself. It is not an hour of deep prayer, nor a time in which I experience a special closeness to God; it is not a period of serious attentiveness to the divine mysteries. I wish it were! On the contrary, it is full of distractions, inner restlessness, sleepiness, confusion, and boredom. It seldom, if ever, pleases my senses. But the simple fact of being for one hour in the presence of the Lord and of showing him all that I feel, think, sense, and experience, without trying to hide anything, must please him.

Somehow, somewhere, I know that he loves me, even though I do not feel that love as I can feel a human embrace, even though I do not hear a voice as I hear human words of consolation, even though I do not see a smile as I can see a human face. Still the Lord speaks to me, looks at me, and embraces me there, where I am still unable to notice it. The only way I become aware of his presence is in that remarkable desire to return to that quiet chapel and be there without any real satisfaction. Yes, I notice, maybe only retrospectively, that my days and weeks are different days and weeks when they are held together by these regular "useless times."

God is greater than my senses, greater than my thoughts, greater than my heart. I do believe that he touches me in places that are unknown even to myself. I seldom can point directly to these places; but when I feel this inner pull to return again to that hidden hour of prayer, I realize that something is happening that is so deep that it becomes like the riverbed through which the waters can safely flow and find their way to the open sea.

—*¡Gracias!* 69–70

5

Called Together

In community, we listen together inwardly for the voice that calls us the beloved, and then we encourage each other to take risks for love in the world and to be that belovedness for others.

Henri treasured the community of faith that gathers around the table at the Eucharist. He considered the church to be the body of Christ, a communion of saints that transcends time and space. This greater community has had its troubles and its failings, and while Henri advocated a loyal and passionate participation in the Roman Catholic Church, he also invited its members to participate in it with some circumspection — to be in it but not of it. We are never free from the need to listen deeply and with delicate discernment to the dynamic, changing form of Christ within ourselves and our communities.

EUCHARIST

Taking Responsibility

The word "Eucharist" means literally "act of thanksgiving." To celebrate the Eucharist and to live a Eucharistic life has everything to do with gratitude. Living Eucharistically is living life as a gift, a gift for which one is grateful. But gratitude is not the most obvious response to life, certainly not when we experience life as a series of losses! Still, the great mystery we celebrate in the Eucharist and live in a Eucharistic life is precisely that through mourning our losses we come to know life as a gift. The beauty and preciousness of life is intimately linked with its fragility and mortality. We can experience that every day — when we take a flower in our hands, when we see a butterfly dance in the air, when we caress a little baby. Fragility and giftedness are both there, and our joy is connected with both.

Each Eucharist begins with a cry for God's mercy. There is probably no prayer in the history of Christianity that has been prayed so frequently and intimately as the prayer "Lord, have mercy." It is the prayer that not only stands at the beginning of all Eucharistic liturgies of the West but also sounds as an ongoing cry through all Eastern liturgies. Lord, have mercy, *Kyrie Eleison, Gospody Pomiloe*. It's the cry of God's people, the cry of people with a contrite heart.

This cry for mercy is possible only when we are willing to confess that somehow, somewhere, we ourselves have something to do with our losses. Crying for mercy is a recognition that blaming God, the world, or others for our losses does not do full justice to the truth of who we are. At the moment we are willing to take responsibility, even for the pain we didn't cause directly; blaming is converted into an acknowledgment of our own role in human brokenness....

Celebrating the Eucharist requires that we stand in this world accepting our co-responsibility for the evil that surrounds and pervades us. As long as we remain stuck in our complaints about the terrible times in which we live and the terrible situations we have to bear and the terrible fate we have to suffer, we can never come to contrition....

Indeed, the conflicts in our personal lives as well as the conflicts on regional, national, or world scales are *our* conflicts, and only by claiming responsibility for them can we move beyond them — choosing a life of forgiveness, peace, and love.

The *Kyrie Eleison* — Lord, have mercy — must emerge from a contrite heart. In contrast to a hardened heart, a contrite heart is a heart that does not blame but acknowledges its own part in the sinfulness of the world and so has been made ready to receive God's mercy.   — *With Burning Hearts,* 30–32

God with Us

The Eucharist is the most ordinary and the most divine gesture imaginable. That is the truth of Jesus. So human, yet so divine; so familiar, yet so mysterious; so close, yet so revealing! But that is the story of Jesus who "being in the form of God did not count equality with God something to be grasped, but emptied himself, taking the form of a slave, becoming as human beings are; and being in every way like a human being, he was humbler yet, even to accepting death, death on a cross" (Phil. 2:18). It is the story of God who wants to come close to us, so close that we can see him with our own eyes, hear him with our own ears, touch him with our own hands; so close that there is nothing between us and him, nothing that separates, nothing that divides, nothing that creates distance.

Jesus is God-for-us, God-with-us, God-within-us. Jesus is God giving himself completely, pouring himself out for us without reserve. Jesus doesn't hold back or cling to his own possessions. He gives all there is to give. "Eat, drink, this is my body, this is my blood . . . this is me for you!" We all know of this desire to give ourselves at the table. We say: "Eat and drink; I made this for you. Take more; it is there for you to enjoy, to be strengthened, yes, to feel how much I love you." What we desire is not simply to give food, but to give ourselves. "Be my guest," we say. And as we encourage our friends to eat from our table, we want to say, "Be my friend, be my companion, be my love — be part of my life — I want to give myself to you."

In the Eucharist, Jesus gives all. The bread is not simply a sign of his desire to become our food; the cup is not just a sign of his willingness to be our drink. Bread and wine *become* his body and blood in the giving. The bread, indeed, is his body given for us; the wine his blood poured out for us. As God becomes fully present for us in Jesus, so Jesus becomes fully present to us in the bread and the wine of the Eucharist. God not only became flesh for us years ago in a country far away. God also becomes food and drink for us now at this moment of the Eucharistic celebration, right where we are together around the table.

God does not hold back; God gives all. That is the mystery of the incarnation. That too is the mystery of the Eucharist. Incarnation and Eucharist are the two expressions of the immense, self-giving love of God. And so the sacrifice on the cross and the sacrifice at the table are one sacrifice, one complete, divine self-giving that reaches out to all humanity in time and space.

— *With Burning Hearts*, 67–69

Held in Not Seeing

Here we touch one of the most sacred aspects of the Eucharist: the mystery that the deepest communion with Jesus is a communion that happens in his absence....

All during his time with the disciples there had been no full communion. Yes, they had stayed with him and sat at his feet; yes, they had been his disciples, even his friends. But they had not yet entered into full communion with him. His body and blood and their body and blood had not yet become one. In many ways, he still had been the other, the one over there, the one who goes ahead of them and shows them the way. But when they eat the bread he gives them and they recognize him, that recognition is a deep spiritual awareness that, now, he dwells in their innermost being, that, now, he breathes in them, speaks in them, yes, lives in them. When they eat the bread that he hands them, their lives are transformed into his life. It is no longer they who live, but Jesus, the Christ, who lives in them. And right at that most sacred moment of communion, he has vanished from their sight.

This is what we live in the Eucharistic celebration. This too is what we live when we live a Eucharistic life. It is a communion so intimate, so holy, so sacred, and so spiritual that our corporeal senses can no longer reach it. No longer can we see him with our mortal eyes, hear him with our mortal ears, or touch him with our mortal bodies. He has come to us at that place within us where the powers of darkness and evil cannot reach, where death has no access.

When he reaches out to us and puts the bread in our hands and brings the cup to our lips, Jesus asks us to let go of the easier

friendship we have had with him so far and to let go of the feelings, emotions, and even thoughts that belong to that friendship.
When we eat of his body and drink of his blood, we accept the
loneliness of not having him any longer at our table as a consoling partner in our conversation, helping us to deal with the losses
of our daily life. It is the loneliness of the spiritual life, the loneliness of knowing that he is closer to us than we ever can be to
ourselves. It's the loneliness of faith.

We will keep crying out, "Lord, have mercy"; we will keep
listening to the Scriptures and their meaning; we will keep saying,
"Yes, I believe." But communion with him goes far beyond all of
that. It brings us to the place where the light blinds our eyes and
where our whole being is wrapped in not-seeing. It is at that place
of communion that we cry out: "God, my God, why have you
abandoned me?" It is at that place, too, that our emptiness gives
us the prayer: "Father, into your hands I commend my Spirit."

— *With Burning Hearts*, 72–74

Our Body, Christ's Body

Today is the feast of Corpus Christi, the body of Christ. As Ed-
ward Malloy, a visiting Holy Cross priest, Don, and I celebrated
the Eucharist in the little Chapel of the Holy Cross house in
Berkeley, the importance of this feast touched me more than ever.
The illness that has severely impaired Don's movements made
him, and also me, very conscious of the beauty, intricacy, and
fragility of the human body. My visit yesterday to the Castro
district, where physical pleasure is so visibly sought and bodily
pain so dramatically suffered, reminded me powerfully that I not
only have a body, but also am a body. The way one lives in the
body, the way one relates to, cares for, exercises, and uses one's
own and other people's bodies, is of crucial importance for one's
spiritual life.

The greatest mystery of the Christian faith is that God came to
us in the body, suffered with us in the body, rose in the body, and
gave us his body as food. No religion takes the body as seriously

as the Christian religion. The body is not seen as the enemy or as a prison of the spirit, but celebrated as the spirit's temple.

Through Jesus' birth, life, death, and resurrection, the human body has become part of the life of God. By eating the body of Christ, our own fragile bodies are becoming intimately connected with the risen Christ and thus prepared to be lifted up with him into the divine life. Jesus says, "I am the living bread which has come down from heaven. Anyone who eats this bread will live forever; and the bread that I shall give is my flesh, for the life of the world" (John 6:51).

It is in union with the body of Christ that I come to know the full significance of my own body. My body is much more than a mortal instrument of pleasure and pain. It is a home where God wants to manifest the fullness of the divine glory. This truth is the most profound basis for the moral life. The abuse of the body — whether it be psychological (e.g., instilling fear), physical (e.g., torture), economic (e.g., exploitation), or sexual (e.g., hedonistic pleasure seeking) — is a distortion of true human destiny: to live in the body eternally with God. The loving care given to our bodies and the bodies of others is therefore a truly spiritual act, since it leads the body closer toward its glorious existence.

I wonder how I can bring this good news to the many people for whom their body is little more than an unlimited source of pleasure or an unceasing source of pain. The feast of the body of Christ is given to us to fully recognize the mystery of the body and to help us find ways to live reverently and joyfully in the body in expectation of the risen life with God.

— *The Road to Daybreak*, 201–2

Earth's Bread and Wine

It is not so difficult to understand why, through all the ages, people searching for the meaning of life tried to live as close to nature as possible. Not only St. Benedict, St. Francis, and St. Bruno in the olden days, but also Thomas Merton, who lived in the woods of Kentucky, and the Benedictine monks, who built their monastery in an isolated canyon in New Mexico. It is not so strange that many young people are leaving the cities and going out into the country to find peace by listening to the voices of nature. And nature indeed speaks: the birds to St. Francis, the trees to the Indians, the river to Siddhartha. And the closer we come to nature, the closer we touch the core of life when we celebrate. Nature makes us aware of the preciousness of life. Nature tells us that life is precious not only because it is, but also because it does not have to be.

I remember sitting day after day at the same table in a dull restaurant where I had to eat my lunch. There was a beautiful red rose in a small vase in the middle of the table. I looked at the rose with sympathy and enjoyed its beauty. Every day I talked with my rose. But then I became suspicious. Because while my mood was changing during the week from happy to sad, from disappointed to angry, from energetic to apathetic, my rose was always the same. And moved by my suspicion I lifted my fingers to the rose and touched it. It was a plastic thing! I was deeply offended and never went back there to eat.

We cannot talk with plastic nature because it cannot tell us the real story about life and death. But if we are sensitive to the voice of nature, we might be able to hear sounds from a world where humans and nature both find their shape. We will never fully understand the meaning of the sacramental signs of bread and wine when they do not make us realize that the whole of nature is a sacrament pointing to a reality far beyond itself....

What happens during a Sunday celebration can be a real celebration only when it reminds us in the fullest sense of what continually happens every day in the world which surrounds us. Bread is more than bread; wine is more than wine: it is God with us — not as an isolated event once a week but as the concentration of a mystery about which all of nature speaks day and night....

If we become more and more aware of the voices of all that surrounds us and grow in respect and reverence for nature, then we also will be able to truly care for ourselves as human beings embedded in nature like a sapphire in a golden ring.

— *Creative Ministry,* 101–3

A Eucharistic Prayer (on the Feast of Corpus Christi)

Dear Lord, on this day dedicated to the Eucharist, I think of the thousands of people suffering from lack of food and of the millions suffering from lack of love. While I am well fed and well cared for, while I am enjoying the fruits of the earth and the love of the brothers, I am aware of the physical and emotional destitution of so many of my fellow human beings.

Isn't my faith in your presence in the breaking of the bread meant to reach out beyond the small circle of my brothers to the larger circle of humanity and to alleviate suffering as much as possible?

If I can recognize you in the Sacrament of the Eucharist, I must also be able to recognize you in the many hungry men, women, and children. If I cannot translate my faith in your presence under the appearance of bread and wine into action for the world, I am still an unbeliever.

I pray therefore, Lord, deepen my faith in your Eucharistic presence and help me find ways to let this faith bear fruit in the lives of many. Amen.   — *A Cry for Mercy*, 72

COMMUNITY

Beyond Individualism

Much of our isolation is self-chosen. We do not like to be dependent on others and, whenever possible, we try to show ourselves that we are in control of the situation and can make our own decisions. This self-reliance has many attractions. It gives us a sense of power, it allows us to move quickly, it offers us the satisfaction of being our own boss, and it promises many rewards and prizes. However, the underside of this self-reliance is loneliness, isolation, and a constant fear of not making it in life.

I have experienced the rewards as well as the punishments of individualism. As a university professor, I was a productive and popular teacher and made it through the many hoops of academic promotion, but at the very end of it all, I felt quite alone.

Notwithstanding all the praise I was receiving while speaking about community, I didn't feel that I truly belonged to anyone. While showing convincingly the importance of prayer, I myself lost the ability to be quiet enough to pray. While encouraging mutual vulnerability as a way to grow in the Spirit, I found myself quite careful and even defensive where my own reputation was at stake. The bottom line for academics is competition — even for those who preach compassion — at least when they don't want to lose their jobs!

To make compassion the bottom line of life, to be open and vulnerable to others, to make community life the focus, and to let prayer be the breath of your life — that requires a willingness to tear down the countless walls that we have erected between ourselves and others in order to maintain our safe isolation. This is a lifelong and arduous spiritual battle because while tearing down walls with one hand, we build new ones with the other. After I had left the university and chosen a life in community, I realized that, even in community, there are numerous ways to play the controlling games of individualism. Indeed, true conversion asks for a lot more than a change of place. It asks for a change of heart.   — Here and Now, 42

A Mosaic of Christ

Community is like a large mosaic. Each little piece seems so insignificant. One piece is bright red, another cold blue or dull green, another warm purple, another sharp yellow, another shining gold. Some look precious, others ordinary. Some look valuable, others worthless. Some look gaudy, others delicate. As individual stones, we can do little with them except compare them and judge their beauty and value. When, however, all these little stones are brought together in one big mosaic portraying the face of Christ, who would ever question the importance of any one of them? If one of them, even the least spectacular one, is missing, the face is incomplete. Together in the one mosaic, each little stone is indispensable and makes a unique contribution to the glory of God. That's community, a fellowship of little people who together make God visible in the world.

Lifting our lives to others happens every time we speak or act in ways that make our lives for others. When we are fully able to embrace our own lives, we discover that what we claim we also want to proclaim. A life well held is indeed a life for others. We stop wondering whether our life is better or worse than others and start seeing clearly that when we live our life for others we not only claim our individuality but also proclaim our unique place in the mosaic of the human family.

— *Can You Drink the Cup?* 58

Joy in Belonging

The movement flowing from the Eucharist is the movement from communion to community to ministry. Our experience of communion first sends us to our brothers and sisters to share with them our stories and build with them a body of love. Then as community, we can move in all directions and reach out to all people.

I am deeply aware of my own tendency to want to go from communion to ministry without forming community. My individualism and desire for personal success ever and again tempt me to do it alone and to claim the task of ministry for myself. But Jesus himself didn't preach and heal alone. Luke the Evangelist tells us how he spent the night in communion with God, the morning to form community with the twelve apostles, and the afternoon to go out with them ministering to the crowds.

Jesus calls us to the same sequence: from communion to community to ministry. He does not want us to go out alone. He sends us out together, two by two, never by ourselves. And so we can witness as people who belong to a body of faith. We are sent out to teach, to heal, to inspire, and to offer hope to the world — not as the exercise of our unique skill, but as the expression of our faith that all we have comes from him who brought us together. — *With Burning Hearts*, 87–88

What Can We Give?

Our life itself is the greatest gift to give — something we constantly forget. When we think about our being given to each other, what comes immediately to mind are our unique talents: those abilities to do special things especially well. You and I have spoken about this quite often. "What is our unique talent?" we asked. However, when focusing on talents, we tend to forget that our real gift is not so much what we can do, but who we *are*.

The real question is not "What can we offer each other?" but "Who can we *be* for each other?"

— *Life of the Beloved*, 90–91

Loving Deeply

Do not hesitate to love and to love deeply. You might be afraid of the pain that deep love can cause. When those you love deeply reject you, leave you, or die, your heart will be broken. But that should not hold you back from loving deeply. The pain that comes from deep love makes your love ever more fruitful. It is like a plow that breaks the ground to allow the seed to take root and grow into a strong plant.

Every time you experience the pain of rejection, absence, or death, you are faced with a choice. You can become bitter and decide not to love again, or you can stand straight in your pain and let the soil on which you stand become richer and more able to give life to new seeds.

The more you have loved and have allowed yourself to suffer because of your love, the more you will be able to let your heart grow wider and deeper. When your love is truly giving and receiving, those whom you love will not leave your heart even when they depart from you. They will become part of your self and thus gradually build a community within you.

Those you have deeply loved become part of you. The longer you live, there will always be more people to be loved by you and to become part of your inner community. The wider your inner community becomes, the more easily you will recognize your own brothers and sisters in the strangers around you. Those who are alive within you will recognize those who are alive around you. The wider the community of your heart, the wider the community around you. Thus the pain of rejection, absence, and death can become fruitful. Yes, as you love deeply the ground of your heart will be broken more and more, but you will rejoice in the abundance of the fruit it will bear.

— *The Inner Voice of Love,* 59–60

Beyond Safety

It is important to remember that the Christian community is a waiting community, that is, a community which not only creates a sense of belonging but also a sense of estrangement. In the Christian community we say to each other, "We are together, but we cannot fulfill each other...we help each other, but we also have to remind each other that our destiny is beyond our togetherness." The support of the Christian community is a support in common expectation. That requires a constant criticism of anyone who makes the community into a safe shelter or a cozy clique and a constant encouragement to look forward to what is to come.

The basis of the Christian community is not the family tie, or social or economic equality, or shared oppression or complaint, or mutual attraction, but the divine call. The Christian community is not the result of human efforts. God has made us into his people by calling us out of "Egypt" to the "New Land," out of the desert to fertile ground, out of slavery to freedom, out of our sin to salvation, out of captivity to liberation. All these words and images give expression to the fact that the initiative belongs to God and that he is the source of our new life together.

It is quite understandable that in our large anonymous cities we look for people on our "wave length" to form small communities. Prayer groups, Bible-study clubs, and house churches, all are ways of restoring or deepening our awareness of belonging to the people of God. But sometimes a false type of like-mindedness can narrow our sense of community. We all should have the

mind of Jesus Christ, but we do not all have to have the mind
of a schoolteacher, a carpenter, a bank director, a congressman,
or whatever socioeconomic or political group. There is a great
wisdom hidden in the old bell tower calling people with very different backgrounds away from their homes to form one body in
Jesus Christ. It is precisely by transcending the many individual
differences that we can become witnesses of God who allows his
light to shine upon poor and rich, healthy and sick alike. But
it is also in this encounter on the way to God that we become
aware of our neighbor's needs and begin to heal each other's
wounds....

Not without reason the church is called a "pilgrim church,"
always moving forward.   — *Reaching Out*, 110–11

The L'Arche Light

The world is waiting for new saints, ecstatic men and women
who are so deeply rooted in the love of God that they are free
to envision a new international order — where justice reigns and
war is no longer the preferred way to solve conflicts among
nations.

Here and there, we catch a glimpse of this vision. When Jean
Vanier took two handicapped people into his house twenty years
ago, he did something that many considered a waste of time and
talent. But for him it became the concrete way from fear to love.
He believed that in choosing the broken as his family, he followed the way of Jesus. Impractical, sentimental, naive? Would
it not have been better for him to devote his energy and talent
to the burning issues of our time? He himself simply did what he
felt called to do, but today, twenty years later, young men and
women from all over the world are working together in countless
homes to care for handicapped people. L'Arche is certainly not a
new international order, nor the end of wars and violence, nor
the beginning of a new foreign policy. But it is a light "put on
the lamp stand where it shines for everyone in the house" (Matt.
5:16). Jean Vanier does not want the light of L'Arche kept under
a basket....

L'Arche reminds us that a worldwide movement of care for the poor and the oppressed can engender a new consciousness which transcends the boundaries of sex, religion, race, and nation. Such a consciousness can give birth to a world community, a community to celebrate our shared humanity, to sing a joyful song of praise to the God of love, and to proclaim the ultimate victory of life over death. — *Lifesigns,* 114, 116

Limited and Unlimited Love

Community is characterized by two things: one is forgiveness, the other is celebration. Forgiveness means that I continually am willing to forgive the other person for not being God — for not fulfilling all my needs. I, too, must ask forgiveness for not being able to fulfill other people's needs.

Our heart — the center of our being — is a part of God. Thus, our heart longs for satisfaction, for total communion. But human beings, whether it's your husband, or your wife, or your father, or your mother, your brother, sister, or child, they are all so limited in giving that which we crave. Since we want so much and we get only part of what we want, we have to keep on forgiving people for not giving us all we want. So I forgive you since you can only love me in a limited way. I forgive my mother that she is not everything I would like her to be. I forgive my father. This is of enormous importance right now because constantly people look to blame their parents, the church, and their friends for not giving them what they need. So many are so angry. They cannot forgive people for offering only limited expressions of an unlimited love. God's love is unlimited but people's love is not. If you enter into any relationship in communion, friendship, marriage, community, the relationships are always riddled with frustration and disappointments. So forgiveness becomes the word for love in the human context.

The interesting thing is that when you can forgive people for not being God then you can celebrate that they are a reflection of God. You can say, "Since you are not God, I love you because you have such beautiful gifts of his love." You don't have everything of God, but what you have to offer is worth celebrating.

By celebrate I mean to lift up, affirm, confirm, to rejoice in another person's gifts. You can say you are a reflection of that unlimited love. That is why community becomes important. . . .

So celebration becomes important and can be very concrete expressions of love, like birthday celebrations that simply say, "I'm happy you are there." It *doesn't* mean lifting up people's talents like "You're a good piano player." [Rather] I lift up your gifts of joy, peace, love, perseverance, kindness, gentleness. We lift up the gifts of the spirit — and these are the reflections of God.

. . . If you look at that passage in Luke, Jesus' community is named one by one, and at the end it says, "Judas Iscariot, who became a traitor." So you see, as soon as you have community, you have a problem. Someone once said that "community is the place where the person you least want to live with always lives." I mean there is always that one person. To be a traitor means to "hand over." It doesn't so much mean betrayal. There is always someone in the community who hands you over to something. It's not just one person. He may be my Judas, you may be another's Judas. It's not that one person in the community is the problem; it's more that different people are handing other people over to suffering all the time without even wanting to. There is always someone who doesn't satisfy my need or someone who irritates me. In every community — whether family or congregation — there is always someone who for someone else is a hair shirt, but that is essential for community. It may not be that we want it, but it is always there. It is not the sentimental life that we want community to be where everybody loves each other. That's never going to be there. People have to be trained to realize that community doesn't mean emotional, affective, total harmony. That's not even good, for we are always on the way, on the move. Imagine if community were all we want it to be, we'd never want to go anywhere. We are a people on the road.

— "Parting Words," 10–13

THE CHURCH

The Body of Christ

Listen to the church. I know that that isn't a popular bit of advice at a time and in a country where the church is frequently seen more as an "obstacle in the way" rather than as "the way" to Jesus. Nevertheless, I'm profoundly convinced that the greatest spiritual danger for our times is the separation of Jesus from the church.

The church is the body of the Lord. Without Jesus there can be no church; and without the church we cannot stay united with Jesus. I've yet to meet anyone who has come closer to Jesus by forsaking the church. To listen to the church is to listen to the Lord of the church. Specifically, this means taking part in the church's liturgical life.... The Eucharist is the heart of the church's life.   — *Letters to Marc*, 75–76

A Communion of Saints

Our society encourages individualism. We are constantly made to believe that everything we think, say, or do is our personal accomplishment, deserving individual attention. But as people who belong to the communion of saints, we know that anything of spiritual value is not the result of individual accomplishment but the fruit of a communal life.

Whatever we know about God and God's love, whatever we know about Jesus — his life, death, and resurrection — whatever we know about the church and its ministry, is not the invention of our minds asking for an award. It is the knowledge that has come to us through the ages from the people of Israel and the prophets, from Jesus and the saints, and from all who have played roles in the formation of our hearts. True spiritual knowledge belongs to the communion of saints.

— *Bread for the Journey*, November 14

The Poor at the Center

The poor are the center of the church. But who are the poor? At first we might think of people who are not like us: people who live in slums, people who go to soup kitchens, people who sleep on the streets, people in prisons, mental hospitals, and nursing homes. But the poor can be very close. They can be in our own families, churches, or workplaces. Even closer, the poor can be our selves, who feel unloved, rejected, ignored, or abused.

It is precisely when we see and experience poverty — whether far away, close by, or in our own hearts — that we need to become the church, that is, hold hands as brothers and sisters, confess our own brokenness and need, forgive one another, heal one another's wounds, and gather around the table of Jesus for the breaking of the bread. Thus, as the poor we recognize Jesus, who became poor for us.

— Bread for the Journey, November 2

Spotless and Tainted

The church is holy *and* sinful, spotless *and* tainted. The church is the bride of Christ, who washed her in cleansing water and took her to himself "with no speck or wrinkle or anything like that, but holy and faultless" (Eph. 5:26–27). The church too is a group of sinful, confused, anguished people constantly tempted by the powers of lust and greed and always entangled in rivalry and competition.

When we say that the church is a body, we refer not only to the holy and faultless body made Christ-like through baptism and Eucharist but also to the broken bodies of all the people who are its members. Only when we keep both these ways of thinking and speaking together can we live in the church as true followers of Jesus.   *— Bread for the Journey,* October 17

A Forgiven, Forgiving Church

If the Pope would just say a few more times in his sermons that the church has been so oppressive over the centuries, it would be such a relief. But we keep trying to defend ourselves. It makes no sense to defend the Crusades, or to defend [our treatment of] Galileo, or to defend [our inadequate response to] the pogroms. Nobody has any need for that. It's not just individuals who need to forgive and be forgiven. We all need to be forgiven. We ask each other to put ourselves in that vulnerable position — and that's when community can be created.

— "Parting Words," 17–18

Being in the Church, Not of It

Often we hear the remark that we have to live *in* the world without being *of* the world. But it may be more difficult to be *in* the church without being *of* the church. Being *of* the church means being so preoccupied by and involved in the many ecclesial affairs and clerical "ins and outs" that we are no longer focused on Jesus. The church then blinds us to what we came to see and deafens us to what we came to hear. Still, it is *in* the church that Christ dwells, invites us to his table, and speaks to us words of eternal love.

Being *in* the church without being *of* it is a great spiritual challenge. — *Bread for the Journey,* October 23

6

Called into the World

This final section illuminates Henri's vision of ministry, both in our local faith communities and also in the larger society. Engagement in the world flows naturally out of personal solitude, prayer, and the Eucharist. The acceptance of our unique belovedness in God brings an overflow of love that naturally wants to address larger social evils such as poverty, injustice, and other forms of suffering that humans inflict upon each other, along with the sufferings of illness, accident, and death.

While Henri gave many years of his life to the training of ordained clergy, and though he envisioned a special role for them, he held all Christians, both ordained and lay, equally responsible as bearers of the Good News that each person is the beloved of God. No follower of Christ is exempt from the invitation to fully manifest the love of Christ. In our ministries, we are called to a life of hospitality and fruitfulness (not necessarily productivity), to participate in the giving and receiving of God's love, and to empower our friends to go out and to be Christ's healing presence for others.

Henri's compassion for those who suffer led him to dark, dangerous, and destitute places all over the world. The selected excerpts here show his concern for two mistakes that compassionate Christians can make when considering the wider world's ills. On the one extreme, some prayerful people become paralyzed by all the suffering they see and withdraw into a purely personal spirituality. At the other extreme, some Christians become social activists whose inner life with God gradually becomes over-

shadowed by moral outrage, righteous indignation, and political strategizing — attitudes and behaviors that eclipse their vulnerability in God. Genuine compassion must never become unmoored from Christ's intimate presence to us in prayer.

Henri Nouwen's writings reflect his commitment to pray with Christians of all denominations, races, and classes, to move toward the suffering margins of societies, and to share the Good News of God's love. His nearly forty books never move far away from his very personal, and often raw, testimonies of struggle along the way to celebrating our oneness as children of God. These selections are offered in humble gratitude for Henri's extraordinary commitment, courage, and love.

MINISTRY

Ordination

Do the priest and the minister have any peculiar gift which they can share? Do they have a vision they can offer to help others see? Are they any closer than anyone else to the source of their existence, and do they know, feel, and see more deeply the condition in which we are imprisoned but from which we want to become free?

If the answer is no, we may rightly wonder if they will ever be able to help us celebrate life. They who are set apart to lead people to the heart of God's mystery will never be able to do so if they are blind, do not know the way, or are afraid to approach the throne of God.

Ordination means the recognition and affirmation of the fact that someone has gone beyond the walls of fear, lives in intimate contact with the God of the living, and has a burning desire to show others the way to God. Ordination does not make anybody anything but is the solemn recognition of the fact that this person has been able to be obedient to God, to hear God's voice and understand God's call, and that he or she can offer others the way to that same experience. Therefore, the minister who wants to make celebration possible is a person of prayer. Only people of prayer can lead others to celebration because everyone who comes in contact with them realizes that they draw their powers from a source they cannot easily locate but they know is strong and deep. The freedom that gives them a certain independence is not authoritarian or distant. Rather, it makes them rise above the immediate needs and most urgent desires of the people around them. They are deeply moved by things happening around them, but they don't allow themselves to be crushed by these things. They listen attentively, speak with a self-evident authority, but do not easily get excited or nervous. In all they say or do, they express the guiding vision of their life. To that vision they are obedient. It makes them distinguish sharply between what is important and what is not. They are not insensitive to what excites people, but they evaluate their needs differently by seeing them in the perspective of the vision. They are happy and content when people listen, but they do not want to form cliques. They do not attach themselves to anybody exclusively. What they say sounds convincing and obvious, but they do not force their opinion on anybody and are not irritated when people do not accept their ideas. . . .

But they also have an inner freedom in respect to this ideal. They know they will not see their purpose realized, and they consider themselves only as a guide to it. They are impressively free toward their own lives. From their actions it becomes clear that they consider their own existence of secondary importance. They do not live to keep themselves alive but to build a new world of which they have already seen the first images and which so appeals to them that the borderline between their life and their death loses its definitiveness. This is someone who not only celebrates life but can also help others desire to do the same.

— *Creative Ministry*, 105–7
(pronouns changed for inclusivity)

Lay Down Our Lives

If there is any sentence in the Gospel that expresses in a very con-centrated way everything I have tried to say . . . , it is the sentence spoken by Jesus to his Apostles the day before his death: "A man can have no greater love than to lay down his life for his friends" (John 15:13).

For me these words summarize the meaning of all Christian ministry. If teaching, preaching, individual pastoral care, organizing, and celebrating are acts of service that go beyond the level of professional expertise, it is precisely because in these acts the minister is asked to lay down his own life for his friends. There are many people who, through long training, have reached a high level of competence in terms of the understanding of human behavior, but few who are willing to lay down their own lives for others and make their weakness a source of creativity.

For many individuals professional training means power. But the minister, who takes off his clothes to wash the feet of his friends, is powerless, and his training and formation are meant to enable him to face his own weakness without fear and make it available to others. It is exactly this creative weakness that gives the ministry its momentum.

Teaching becomes ministry when the teacher moves beyond the transference of knowledge and is willing to offer his own life experience to his student so that paralyzing anxiety can be removed, new liberating insight can come about, and real learning can take place. Preparing becomes mystery when the preacher moves beyond the "telling of the story" and makes his own deepest self available to his hearers so that they will be able to receive the Word of God. Individual care becomes ministry when he who wants to be of help moves beyond the careful balance of give and take with a willingness to risk his own life and remain faithful to his suffering fellow man even when his own name and fame is in danger. Organizing becomes ministry when the organizer moves beyond his desire for concrete results and looks at his world with the unwavering hope for a total renewal. Celebrating becomes ministry when the celebrant moves beyond the limits of protective rituals to an obedient acceptance of life as a gift.

Although none of these tasks of service can ever be fulfilled without careful preparation and proved competence, none can ever be called ministry when this competence is not grounded in

the radical commitment to lay down one's own life in the service
of others. Ministry means the ongoing attempt to put one's own
search for God, with all the moments of pain and joy, despair
and hope, at the disposal of those who want to join this search
but do not know how. Therefore, ministry in no way is a privilege. Instead, it is the core of the Christian life. No Christian is a
Christian without being a minister.... Whatever form the Christian ministry takes, the basis is always the same: to lay down
one's life for one's friends.   — *Creative Ministry,* 110–11

Celibacy

Celibacy has a very important place in our world. The celibate
makes his life into a visible witness for the priority of God in our
lives, a sign to remind all people that without the inner sanctum
our lives lose contact with their source and goal. We belong to
God. All people do. Celibates are people who, by not attaching
themselves to any one particular person, remind us that the relationship with God is the beginning, the source, and the goal of
all human relationships.

By his or her life of nonattachment, the celibate lifts up an aspect of the Christian life of which we all need to be reminded.
The celibate is like the clown in the circus who, between the
scary acts of the trapeze artists and lion tamers, fumbles and
falls, reminding us that all human activities are ultimately not
so important as the virtuosi make us believe. Celibates live out
the holy emptiness in their lives by not marrying, by not trying to
build for themselves a house or a fortune, by not trying to wield
as much influence as possible, and by not filling their lives with
events, people, or creations for which they will be remembered.
They hope that by their empty lives God will be recognized as
the source of all human thoughts and actions. Especially by not
marrying and by abstaining from the most intimate expression
of human love, the celibate becomes a living sign of the limits
of interpersonal relationships and of the centrality of the inner
sanctum that no human being may violate.

To whom, then, is this witness directed? I dare to say that

celibacy is, first of all, a witness to all those who are married. I wonder if we have explored enough the very important relationship between marriage and celibacy. Lately we have become aware of this interrelatedness in a very painful way. The crisis of celibacy and the crisis of married life appeared together. At the same time that many priests and religious persons move away from the celibate life, we see many couples questioning the value of their commitment to each other. These two phenomena, although they are not connected with each other as cause and effect, are closely related because marriage and celibacy are two ways of living within the Christian community that support each other. Celibacy is a support to married people in their commitment to each other. The celibate reminds those who live together in marriage of their own celibate center, which they need to protect and nurture in order to live a life that does not depend simply upon the stability of emotions and affections, but also on their common love for God, who called them together.

— Clowning in Rome, 48–49

Preaching Good News

If we say that preaching means announcing the good news, it is important to realize that for most people there is absolutely no news in the sermon. Practically nobody listens to a sermon with the expectation of hearing something they did not already know. They have heard about Jesus — his disciples, his sayings, his miracles, his death and resurrection — at home, in kindergarten, in grade school, in high school, and in college so often and in so many different ways and forms that the last thing they expect to come from a pulpit is any news. And the core of the Gospel — "You must love the Lord your God with all your heart, with all your soul, and with all your mind, and you must love your neighbor as yourself" — has been repeated so often and so persistently that it has lost, for the majority of people, even the slightest possibility of evoking any response. They have heard it from the time of their earliest childhood and will continue to hear it until they are dead — unless, of course, they become so bored on the way that they refuse to place themselves any longer in a situation in which they will be exposed to this redundant information. It is fascinating to see how people sit up straight, eyes wide open, when the preacher starts his sermon with a little secular story by way of appetizer, but immediately turn on their sleeping signs and curl up in a more comfortable position when the famous line comes: "And this, my brothers and sisters, is exactly what Jesus meant when he said . . . " From then on most preachers are alone, relying only on the volume of their voices or the idiosyncrasies of their movements to keep in contact. It is indeed sad to say that the name of Jesus for many people has lost most of its mobilizing power. Too often the situation is like the one in the Catholic school where the teacher asked: "Children, who invented the steam engine?" Everyone was silent until finally a little boy sitting in the back of the class raised his finger and said in a dull voice and with watery eyes: "I guess it is Jesus again."

When a message has become so redundant that it has completely lost the ability to evoke any kind of creative response it can hardly be considered a message any longer. And if you feel you cannot avoid being present physically at its presentation you at least can close your eyes and mind and drop out.

— *Creative Ministry,* 25–26

Ministry as Being-With

Two words that I think are helpful for ministry are "compassion" and "gratitude." Ministry happens when you participate in the mystery of being-with. The whole incarnation, God-with-us, Emmanuel, is first of all being with people. Caring means "to cry out with." Compassion literally means "to be with those who suffer." Ministry means that we lift the incarnation — we lift the God who says, "I will be with you." We are to be precisely where people are vulnerable, not to fix it or to change it. That is an unintended fruit of it, but that is not why we are there.

Compassion is the priesthood of Jesus — read the letter to the Hebrews. Since nothing human was alien to him, he was the compassionate high priest. Jesus is first of all God-with-us. For thirty years he was just living in a small village, living the same life that we live. It was for only three years that he was preaching. So even when you look at it in a spiritual way, Jesus' ministry wasn't just the three years he was preaching. The mystery is that he shared our lives. God is a God-with-us. Ministry is being with the sick, the dying, being with people wherever they are, whatever their problems. We dare to be with them in their weakness and trust that if we are entering into people's vulnerable places, we will experience immense joy. That is the mystery of ministry.

You can't solve the world's problems, but you can be with people. I've been with two people who were dying in the last months. It wasn't a burden — it was a great joy to have the privilege to be there when they made their passage.

If I follow God, I pray, I say certain things, and I tell others in need that I care. But I don't sit down beforehand and plan how to get this person from here to there. If I am not in communion with God or in community with other people, then I become a technician who got involved, but as a technician I cannot lay down my life for my friends. My life is my joy, my peace, and my sorrow. Ministry is witness. It's nothing else but saying, "I've seen something, I've experienced something, and I'm not afraid to share it with you if you ask me to." Ministry doesn't have that quality of compulsiveness that it has to happen right away or if I don't say something at the right time that person will become lost.

— "Parting Words," 14–15

Giving Is Receiving

Mission is not only to go and tell others about the risen Lord, but also to receive that witness from those to whom we are sent. Often mission is thought of exclusively in terms of giving, but true mission is also receiving. If it is true that the Spirit of Jesus blows where it wants, there is no person who cannot give that Spirit. In the long run, mission is possible only when it is as much receiving as giving, as much being cared for as caring. We are sent to the sick, the dying, the handicapped, the prisoners, and the refugees to bring them the good news of the Lord's resurrection.

But we will soon be burned out if we cannot receive the Spirit of the Lord from those to whom we are sent.

That Spirit, the Spirit of love, is hidden in their poverty, brokenness, and grief. That is why Jesus said: "Blessed are the poor, the persecuted, and those who mourn." Each time we reach out to them they in turn — whether they are aware of it or not — will bless us with the Spirit of Jesus and so become our ministers. Without this mutuality of giving and receiving, mission and ministry easily become manipulative or violent. When only one gives and the other receives, the giver will soon become an oppressor and the receivers, victims. But when the giver receives and the receiver gives, the circle of love, begun in the community of the disciples, can grow as wide as the world.

— *With Burning Hearts,* 89

A Ministry of Empowerment

Gratitude is essential to ministry. Gratitude basically means to receive the gifts of others — to say thank you for being you. It is a central part of ministry to receive the gifts of others. Only when you yourself have experienced your own giftedness can you be free. We have a desire to get things to other people so that we can be on the giving side. We forget that the greater joy for other people is for them to realize that they have something to give to us.

I can care for handicapped people my whole life, and they need thousands of things, but the greater joy for other people is to be able to do some things themselves. When I can be excited about them, take them on a lecture tour with me and hear others say to them, "Wow, you were great!" these are gifts. When I take Bill or one of the others from L'Arche with me, it's not to show other people how much I care for them; rather I do it so they can offer something. I'm the mediator of that. I need to be there with them. They cannot give their gifts if I'm not there to make them visible.

For instance, I am leaving New Jersey soon. When I began praying here, the group said, "You're the one who knows all about prayer." Yes, I have a certain sophistication around these things, but if I stayed here longer, they would see that I am not always grateful and things don't always work for me. The point is that, finally, I have to empower people, and say, "You have as much to give as I do." Ministry always means to empower others to give their gifts to each other. Ministry is about multiplication. You give away what you have — that little piece of bread in your hand — and it multiplies. You give away the little ministry that you have and everyone becomes a minister to others. Then there is more ministry being done than you have ever seen.

This is what Jesus meant when he said [in effect], "It is good for you that I die; if I go then you can do your job." Jesus' task was to create a community that was empowered. Jesus said, "I will go and I will send my spirit, and my spirit will empower you. All the things the Father told me, I'm telling you. All the things I am doing, you will do, and even greater things."

Jesus never said that he could do something that we couldn't do. He never said that he was something we are not. He said, I am the son of God, and you are children of God. I am called from death to life and you are as well. I know everything about the love of God and I hold back nothing from you. That's the whole concept of the church; we are the body of Christ — we are the living Christ. The sacramental vision of Christ means that Christ is where we are. Just as Christ went away in order to empower others, every minister has to go away sometimes to empower others. It's good for you that I die, that I go away so that you can claim the gifts of God. But for a while I have to be with you so that you can discover your gifts, but then you have to let me go so that they can fully bloom.

— "Parting Words," 15–17

SOCIAL AND POLITICAL ACTION

The Danger of Withdrawal

Yesterday I shared with John Eudes some of my thoughts about prayer for others. He not only confirmed my thoughts but also led me further by saying that compassion belongs to the center of the contemplative life. When we become the other and so enter into the presence of God, then we are true contemplatives. True contemplatives, then, are not the ones who withdrew from the world to save their own soul, but the ones who enter into the center of the world and pray to God from there.

— *Genesee Diary,* 123

Envisioning a New Order

A Christian is a Christian only when he unceasingly asks critical questions of the society in which he lives and continuously stresses the necessity for conversion, not only of the individual but also of the world. A Christian is a Christian only when he refuses to allow himself or anyone else to settle into a comfortable rest. He remains dissatisfied with the status quo. And he believes that he has an essential role to play in the realization of the new world to come — even if he cannot say how that world will come about. A Christian is a Christian only when he keeps saying to everyone he meets that the good news of the Kingdom has to be proclaimed to the whole world and witnessed to all nations (Matt. 24:13).

As long as a Christian lives he keeps searching for a new order without divisions between people, for a new structure that allows every man to shake hands with every other man, and a new life in which there will be lasting unity and peace. He will not allow his neighbor to stop moving, to lose courage, or to escape into small everyday pleasures to which he can cling. He is irritated by satisfaction and self-content in himself as well as in others since he knows, with an unshakable certainty, that something great is coming of which he has already seen the first rays of light.

He believes that this world not only passes but has to pass in order to let the new world be born. He believes that there will never be a moment in this life in which one can rest in the supposition that there is nothing left to do. But he will not despair when he does not see the result he wanted to see. For in the midst

of all his work he keeps hearing the words of the One sitting on the throne: "I am making the whole of creation new" (Rev. 21:5).
— *Creative Ministry,* 88–89

Creating a New Freedom

Ecstatic living entails a constant willingness to leave the safe, secure, familiar place and to reach out to others, even when that involves risking one's own security. On an international scale this means a foreign policy that goes far beyond the question "How can our nation survive?" It would be a policy primarily concerned with the survival of humanity and willing to make national sacrifices. It would be a policy which realizes that idolizing the security of the nation endangers the whole of humanity. It would be a policy which places being human before being American, Russian, Cuban, Nicaraguan, or Mexican. In short, it would be a policy that seeks to liberate nations from their mutual fear and offers ways to celebrate our common humanity.

Ecstasy always reaches out to new freedom. As long as national security is our primary concern and national survival more important than preserving life on this planet, we continue to live in the house of fear. Ultimately, we must choose between security — individual, social, or national — and freedom.... The life of discipleship goes far beyond individual piety or communal loyalty. The whole world is to be converted! Nations, not just individual people, are called to leave the house of fear — where suspicion, hatred, and war rule — and enter the house of love, where reconciliation, healing, and peace can reign.

The great spiritual leaders, from St. Benedict to St. Catherine of Siena to Martin Luther King, Jr., to Thomas Merton, have all grasped this truth: the power of the renewing Word of God cannot be kept within the safe boundaries of the personal or interpersonal. They call for a new Jerusalem, a new earth, a new global community.

The movement from the house of fear to the house of love has become necessary for the survival of humanity....

We *must* move out of the place of death wishes and death

threats and search, as nations, for ways of international reconciliation, cooperation, and care. We indeed need academies of
peace, ministries of peace, and peacekeeping forces. We need educational reform, church reform, and even entertainment reform
that makes peace its main concern. We need a new economic
order beyond socialism and capitalism which makes justice for
all its goal. But most of all, we need to believe as nations that a
new international order is possible and that the rivalries between
countries or blocs of countries are as outdated as the medieval
rivalries between cities. This is what "global ecstasy" is all about.
It is the movement from fear to love, from death to life, from
stagnation to rebirth, from living as rivals to living as people who
belong to one human community.   —*Lifesigns*, 109, 112–13

The World in Our Hearts

It is tragic to see how the religious sentiment of the West has become so individualized that concepts such as a "contrite heart,"
have come to refer only to personal experiences of guilt and the
willingness to do penance for it. The awareness of our impurity
in thoughts, words, and deeds can indeed put us in a remorse-
ful mood and create in us the hope for a forgiving gesture. But if
the catastrophic events of our days, the wars, mass murders, un-
bridled violence, crowded prisons, torture chambers, the hunger
and illness of millions of people, and the unnameable misery of
a major part of the human race are safely kept outside the solitude of our hearts, our contrition remains no more than a pious
emotion.   —*Reaching Out*, 37

Spiritual Colonialism

This is my last day in Cuzco [Peru]. John, Kathy, and I made a
trip to the splendid Inca ruins in the area and to some churches
and a museum in town. More than ever before, I was impressed
by the majestic beauty of the buildings of the Inca empire. The
gigantic temples, the watchposts, and the ritual baths were the
work of a people guided by the rule, "Do not lie, do not steal,

and do not be lazy," and inspired by a powerful devotion to the Sun God and many other divinities. But, more than before, I was stunned by the total insensitivity of the Spanish conquerors to the culture and religion they found here.

It suddenly hit me how radical Gustavo Gutiérrez's liberation theology really is, because it is a theology that starts with the people and wants to recognize the deep spirituality of the Indians who live in this land. How different from what we saw today on our trip. There we witnessed a centuries-long disregard for any Indian religiosity and a violent destruction of all that could possibly be a reminder of the Inca Gods. What an incredible pretension, what a cruelty, what a sacrilegious sin committed by people who claimed to come in the name of a God of forgiveness, love, and peace.

I wished I had the time to spend a whole day just sitting on the ruins of Sacsahuaman. These temple ruins overlooking the city of Cuzco, with its many churches built from its stones, make me ask the God of the sun, the moon, the stars, the rainbow, the lightning, the land, and the water to forgive what Christians did in his name.

Maybe the new spirituality of liberation is a creative form of repentance for the sins of our fathers. And I should not forget that these sins are closer to my own heart than I often want to confess. Some form of spiritual colonialism remains a constant temptation.   —*¡Gracias!* 178–79

The Temptation of Invulnerability

Everyone who wants to change society is in danger of putting himself above it and being more conscious of the weaknesses of others than of the weakness in his own soul. The reformer, who is convinced that things have to become different, is out to convert the world but is tempted at the same time to think that he himself does not need conversion. Instead of seeing himself as a full member of that same society which needs reform, he might approach it with the fantasy of a redeemer who himself is untouchable and is always right and just.

He might see the cruel segregation between races but be blind to the fact that what he sees dramatically happening on the world scene is also happening in himself when he condemns certain people as being stupid, others as being narrow-minded, and still others as being conceited. He might be very critical of capitalism and the waste of money but not see that his own style of life would be impossible without the capitalistic society he condemns. He might feel that many people should have a better life and more human respect but at the same time be unable to listen to people, accept their criticism, and believe that he can learn from them. He might always be busy going from one meeting to another and forget that he himself tends to lose contact with the sources of his own existence and become deaf to the voice that calls from within. He might even be afraid to be alone and face the fact that he himself is in just as much need of change as the world he wants to convert.

The three dangers for everyone who is concerned about social change are, therefore, concretism, power, and pride. When Jesus had become aware of his vocation to criticize the society in which he lived, to question its basic supposition, and to work for the Kingdom to come, he knew that he too could have become an organizer in the long row of those who had already called themselves Messiahs. And indeed he was tempted to bring about immediate results and change the stones into bread, to take the power and the glory of all the kingdoms of the world, and to prove his invulnerability by throwing himself down from the parapet of the temple and allowing the angels to guard him.

But only through overcoming these temptations could he become a revolutionary man who was able to break through the narrowing chains of his world and surpass all political ambitions in order to make visible the new Kingdom to come.

— *Creative Ministry,* 75–76

Prayerful Action

Prayer and action can never be seen as contradictory or mutually exclusive. Prayer without action grows into powerless pietism, and action without prayer degenerates into questionable manipulation. If prayer leads us into a deeper unity with the compassionate Christ, it will always give rise to concrete acts of service. And if concrete acts of service do indeed lead us to a deeper solidarity with the poor, the hungry, the sick, the dying, and the oppressed, they will always give rise to prayer. In prayer we meet Christ, and in him all human suffering. In service we meet people, and in them the suffering Christ.

Action with and for those who suffer is the concrete expression of the compassionate life and the final criterion of being a Christian. Such acts do not stand beside the moments of prayer and worship but are themselves such moments. Why? Because Jesus Christ, who did not cling to his divinity, but became as we are, can be found where there are hungry, thirsty, alienated, naked, sick, and imprisoned people. Precisely when we live in an ongoing conversation with Christ and allow his Spirit to guide our lives, we will recognize him in the poor, the oppressed, and the downtrodden and will hear his cry and respond to it wherever he reveals himself.   — *Compassion,* 116–17

MODERN SPIRITUAL MASTERS SERIES

Other volumes in this series are available at your local bookseller or directly through Orbis Books.

Dietrich Bonhoeffer

Writings Selected with an Introduction by Robert Coles

ISBN 1-57075-194-3, $13.00, paperback

Simone Weil

Writings Selected with an Introduction by Eric O. Springsted

ISBN 1-57075-204-4, $13.00, paperback

To place your order with Mastercard and VISA, call toll-free 1-800-258-5838,

E-mail via our Web page at http://www.maryknoll.org/orbis/mklorbhp.htm

or write to: **ORBIS BOOKS**
Walsh Building
P.O. Box 308
Maryknoll, N.Y. 10545-0308

Titles subject to availability. Prices subject to change.